D1544626

Understanding American History

The Salem Witch Trials

Gail B. Stewart

Bruno Leone
Series Consultant

ReferencePoint Press®

San Diego, CA

© 2013 ReferencePoint Press, Inc.
Printed in the United States

For more information, contact:
ReferencePoint Press, Inc.
PO Box 27779
San Diego, CA 92198
www. ReferencePointPress.com

LIBRARY OF CONGRESS CATALOGING-IN-PUBLICATION DATA

Stewart, Gail B. (Gail Barbara), 1949–
  The Salem witch trials / by Gail Stewart.
     p. cm. -- (Understanding American history)
  Includes bibliographical references and index.
  ISBN-13: 978-1-60152-282-5 (hardback : alk. paper)
  ISBN-10: 1-60152-282-7 (hardback : alk. paper) 1. Trials (Witchcraft)--Massachusetts--
Salem--Juvenile literature. I. Title.
  KFM2478.8.W5S87 2012
  133.4'3097445--dc23
                                                          2011047778

Contents

Foreword   4

Important Events of the Salem Witch Trials   6

Introduction   8
    The Defining Characteristics of the Salem Witch Trials

Chapter One   12
    What Conditions Led to the Salem Witch Trials?

Chapter Two   25
    Murmurs and Accusations

Chapter Three   39
    The Hearings Begin

Chapter Four   53
    Trials and Punishments

Chapter Five   66
    What Is the Legacy of the Salem Witch Trials?

Source Notes   81

Important People of the Salem Witch Trials   86

For Further Research   88

Index   90

Picture Credits   95

About the Author   96

Foreword

America's Puritan ancestors—convinced that their adopted country was blessed by God and would eventually rise to worldwide prominence—proclaimed their new homeland the shining "city upon a hill." The nation that developed since those first hopeful words were uttered has clearly achieved prominence on the world stage and it has had many shining moments but its history is not without flaws. The history of the United States is a virtual patchwork of achievements and blemishes. For example, America was originally founded as a New World haven from the tyranny and persecution prevalent in many parts of the Old World. Yet the colonial and federal governments in America took little or no action against the use of slave labor by the southern states until the 1860s, when a civil war was fought to eliminate slavery and preserve the federal union.

In the decades before and after the Civil War, the United States underwent a period of massive territorial expansion; through a combination of purchase, annexation, and war, its east–west borders stretched from the Atlantic to the Pacific Oceans. During this time, the Industrial Revolution that began in eighteenth-century Europe found its way to America, where it was responsible for considerable growth of the national economy. The United States was now proudly able to take its place in the Western Hemisphere's community of nations as a worthy economic and technological partner. Yet America also chose to join the major western European powers in a race to acquire colonial empires in Africa, Asia, and the islands of the Caribbean and South Pacific. In this scramble for empire, foreign territories were often peacefully annexed but military force was readily used when needed, as in the Philippines during the Spanish-American War of 1898.

Toward the end of the nineteenth century and concurrent with America's ambitions to acquire colonies, its vast frontier and expanding industrial base provided both land and jobs for a new and ever-growing wave of immigrants from southern and eastern Europe. Although America had always encouraged immigration, these newcomers—Italians, Greeks, and eastern European Jews, among others—were seen as different from the vast majority of earlier immigrants, most of whom were from northern and western Europe. The presence of these newcomers was treated as a matter of growing concern, which in time evolved into intense opposition. Congress boldly and with calculated prejudice set out to create a barrier to curtail the influx of unwanted nationalities and ethnic groups to America's shores. The outcome was the National Origins Act, passed in 1924. That law severely reduced immigration to the United States from southern and eastern Europe. Ironically, while this was happening, the Statue of Liberty stood in New York Harbor as a visible and symbolic beacon lighting the way for people of *all* nationalities and ethnicities seeking sanctuary in America.

Unquestionably, the history of the United States has not always mirrored that radiant beacon touted by the early settlers. As often happens, reality and dreams tend to move in divergent directions. However, the story of America also reveals a people who have frequently extended a helping hand to a weary world and who have displayed a ready willingness—supported by a flexible federal constitution—to take deliberate and effective steps to correct injustices, past and present. America's private and public philanthropy directed toward other countries during times of natural disasters (such as the contributions of financial and human resources to assist Haiti following the January 2010, earthquake) and the legal right to adopt amendments to the US Constitution (including the Thirteenth Amendment freeing the slaves and the Nineteenth Amendment granting women the right to vote) are examples of the nation's generosity and willingness to acknowledge and reverse wrongs.

With objectivity and candor, the titles selected for the Understanding American History series portray the many sides of America, depicting both its shining moments and its darker hours. The series strives to help readers achieve a wider understanding and appreciation of the American experience and to encourage further investigation into America's evolving character and founding principles.

Important Events of the Salem Witch Trials

1487
Malleus Maleficarum is published in Germany to help witch-hunters find and execute witches.

1630
Puritans begin farming in Salem Village, a settlement just outside of Salem Town.

1620
The first Puritans arrive in the New World in what is now Massachusetts.

1641
English law makes witchcraft a crime punishable by death.

1487	1625	1640	1690

1626
Puritans found the seaport community of Salem Town.

1688
Thirteen-year-old Martha Goodwin begins acting in a bizarre fashion after an argument with laundress Goody Glover; Cotton Mather publishes *Memorable Providences, Relating to Witchcrafts and Possessions,* his widely read account of an episode of supposed witchcraft involving Goody Glover.

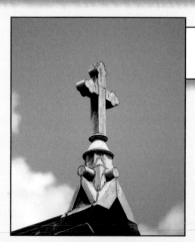

1689
The Reverend Samuel Parris is hired as pastor of Salem Village.

January 1692
Abigail Williams and Betty Parris begin experiencing fits and convulsions that will be blamed on witchcraft.

February 1692
Sarah Good, Sarah Osborne, and Tituba are charged with being witches.

March 1692

Tituba confesses to practicing witchcraft and confirms that Sarah Good and Sarah Osborne are her co-conspirators.

May 1692

Governor William Phips appoints the Court of Oyer and Terminer to try those accused of witchcraft, and Judge Samuel Sewall requests jury members for the new court.

August 1692

Five more accused witches die by the hangman's noose: George Jacobs Sr., Martha Carrier, George Burroughs, John Willard, and John Proctor.

1693

The pending cases are reviewed by the court, and those accused are either dismissed or pardoned once their jail fees are paid.

1692   1693   1694   1695   1696   1697

July 1692

Five people are hanged at Gallows Hill: Rebecca Nurse, Susannah Martin, Sarah Good, Sarah Wildes, and Elizabeth Howe.

1697

Massachusetts declares January 14 a day of repentance to atone for the Salem witch trials.

June 1692

Bridget Bishop becomes the first person hanged for witchcraft in Salem.

October 1692

Increase Mather questions whether spectral evidence should be used in court; Governor William Phips orders the witch trials stopped.

April 1692

After protesting the examination of his wife, Elizabeth, John Proctor becomes the first man accused of and jailed for witchcraft.

September 1692

Giles Corey is pressed to death for refusing to enter a plea; eight more people are hanged.

The Defining Characteristics of the Salem Witch Trials

One of the oddest—and saddest—periods of American history began in late January 1692 in Salem Village, Massachusetts—population about 600. A small number of girls between the ages of nine and 13 began experiencing bizarre fits during which they screamed, cursed, hallucinated, threw things, and contorted their bodies into odd positions. Physicians could find no medical explanation for the girls' outbursts and instead theorized that the girls were under an evil spell. When the afflicted girls began naming certain members of the community who had bewitched them, events soon spiraled out of control.

Over the next 9 months, more began experiencing these fits, and they, too, named other villagers whom they said were witches. Hundreds of people were questioned and tried, and more than 150 suspected witches from Salem Village and two dozen other nearby towns and villages were jailed. Those who were accused of being witches protested their innocence, insisting that they were good Christian people and would never practice witchcraft. Their pleas did not move the judges, however, and by September 1692, 28 had been convicted of witchcraft, 20 were executed, and five died in prison before their trials took place.

A Time of Stress and Uncertainty

The time during which the Salem witch trials occurred was one of al-most unimaginable rigidity in almost every aspect of society. Salem had been founded by people who had brought with them their very strict, fundamentalist religion. They believed in a God who was neither lov-ing nor forgiving, but rather was vengeful and vindictive, constantly watching and judging their every move. Whether man, woman, or small child, they were taught that the slightest mistake, the smallest misstep, could mean the difference between one's going to heaven or burning in hell for all eternity.

Never were they to forget that life was not meant to be happy or enjoyable. As well-known seventeenth-century clergyman Samuel Wil-lard warned his congregation, life was a battle to survive without yield-ing to the devil. "[You] are not to lie upon a bed of ease," he cautioned, "but to engage in a field of war . . . and endure to the end."[1]

This was also a time when people had no real understanding of the natural world. Germs and viruses were unknown, as were the basics of weather science. As a result, they had no scientific explanations for

Massachusetts Circa 1692

frightening events that occurred, whether an outbreak of measles or a flash flood that destroyed farms and homes. Lacking such understanding, says historian Richard Weisman, whenever bad things happened, people viewed them as the logical consequences of God's disapproval. "Crop failures, epidemics, Indian raids, and sundry other disasters were perceived not as accidents or as the mere logical [particulars] of wilderness living, but rather as judgments rendered according to the moral failings of the community. As the national sins increased, so would the severity of divine afflictions."[2]

A Belief in Witches

The void that resulted from the lack of explanations for such natural occurrences was filled with a strong belief in the supernatural, especially witches. The belief in witchcraft and sorcery was commonplace throughout Europe and had been since ancient times.

In 1487 two German Dominican priests published *Malleus Maleficarum* (Latin for "Hammer of Witches"), a 250,000-word witch-hunting manual—a sort of how-to guide detailing the best ways to identify and punish those who practiced witchcraft. It was no secret, the authors maintained, that women were more likely to be caught up in witchcraft, because they were less intelligent than men and therefore less able to resist the temptation of evil spirits. The authors wrote: "What else is woman but a foe to friendship, an unescapable punishment, a necessary evil, a natural temptation, a desirable calamity, a domestic danger, a delectable detriment, an evil of nature, painted with fair colors! . . . We may add . . . that since they are feebler both in mind and body, it is not surprising that they should come more under the spell of witchcraft."[3]

A Legacy of Witch Hunts

Over the next two centuries, zealous witch-hunters throughout Europe followed the book's instructions—with shockingly successful results. During a 15-year period in the Lorraine region of France, for example, attorney general Nicholas Remy identified and condemned more than

900 people he believed to be witches. In Germany 1,500 alleged witches were burned at the stake. According to expert Robin Briggs in his book *Witches and Neighbours*, "The most reasonable modern estimates suggest perhaps 100,000 trials between 1450 and 1750, with something between 40,000 and 50,000 executions."[4]

With such a pervasive fear of witchcraft in Europe, it is not at all surprising that the people who left to start new lives elsewhere brought those same fears with them. No group illustrates that more than the Puritans, the fundamentalist Christians who immigrated to the American colony of Massachusetts in the early seventeenth century. They hoped to achieve the religious freedom they lacked in England, but their arrival marked the beginning of what remains one of the ugliest chapters in American history.

Chapter 1

What Conditions Led to the Salem Witch Trials?

The witch hunts in England and the rest of Europe undoubtedly played a role in the hysteria that fueled the Salem trials. But historians believe that the Puritan way of life—especially the strictness of the Puritan religion and culture—explains far more about the witch frenzy in seventeenth-century Massachusetts than events that took place in the land of the Puritans' birth.

Demands from the Puritans

The people who arrived in Massachusetts in 1626 were members of a splinter group of Protestants known as Puritans. Their form of Christianity began in the 1530s in England. Prior to this time, England and other European countries recognized Catholicism as the official religion. In fact, the authority of the pope in many cases surpassed even that of the king.

But in 1530 King Henry VIII of England wished to divorce his wife—something that went against church teachings. After the pope refused to allow the divorce, Henry became furious and established his own church, which he called the Church of England. The new religion was a denomination of Christianity headed not by a pope but by the English king himself. While the new religion was accepted by most people in England, one group felt it was not strict enough. They had never liked the Catholic Church either, with its use of crucifixes, elaborate rituals, priceless art decorating churches, and the playing of instrumental music during mass, which they considered pompous. Because of their insistence that the newly created Church of England be made "purer"—stricter, more fundamental, and less gaudy—they became known as Puritans.

The Puritans' criticism of the Church of England continued through the years, though they were unsuccessful in their efforts to change it. While they openly declared themselves as God's chosen people, to others they often appeared arrogant and self-righteous—especially in their criticisms of other religions. In fact, when James I became king of England in 1603, he not only refused to listen to their demands, he ordered many of the Puritan ministers fired from their posts within the church. To escape the throne's growing intolerance, Puritans began migrating to the New World in the early seventeenth century.

"We Shall Be as a City upon a Hill"

A small group of Puritans arrived in Plymouth, Massachusetts, in 1620. Over the next 20 years, 15,000 more Puritans followed, settling in Boston, Salem, and other places that would come to be known collectively as the Massachusetts Bay Colony. The Puritans established a theocracy—a religious society whose leaders would govern according to their idea of God's wishes. Instead of having a separation of church and state, the new colony was founded on the idea that the two were virtually the same.

John Winthrop, the leader of a large group that arrived in 1626, expressed an optimistic view of the life the Puritans hoped to build in their new home. He insisted that they should always

> be knit together in this work as one man. We must entertain each other in brotherly affection. We must be willing to abridge ourselves of our superfluities [luxuries], for the supply of other necessities. We must uphold a familiar commerce together in all meekness, gentleness, patience, and liberality. We must delight

in each other, make others' conditions our own, rejoice together, mourn together, labor, and suffer together, always having before our eyes our commission and community in the work. . . . So shall we keep the unity of the spirit in the bond of peace. . . . For we must consider that we shall be as a city upon a hill, the eyes of all people are upon us.[5]

Though they were relieved to escape the religious constraints of England, the Puritans understood that life in the New World would be extremely challenging. The first arrivals settled on the coast and founded the seaport communities of Boston and Salem Town. The Puritans who arrived later found the towns overcrowded and moved inland. They created a separate community, a farming settlement between 5 and 7 miles (8km and 11.3km) north of Salem Town, known as Salem Village. There they looked forward to living the kind of life they wanted—as God's chosen people.

A Difficult Religion

As with all Puritan families, those who settled in Salem Village understood that religion guided every aspect of daily life. Theirs was a rigid, severe belief system that taught that God was always observing them and would punish them for even the most minor mistakes.

For the Puritans life was a constant struggle between the forces of good and evil. Around every corner, they believed, the devil and his minions were lurking, waiting to tempt good people into committing bad acts. Puritans did not believe anything happened by accident. Everything happened for a reason. A storm that ruined crops, a child who became ill, cows that sickened and died—all of these, they believed, were punishments sent to them because of their own mistakes or misdeeds.

They also firmly believed that God preordained every person's fate before he or she was born. No one knew whether specific people were destined for hell or for eternal life in heaven with the godly people. As a result, they were always searching for evidence of God's moods. For

Witches' Familiars

For centuries people believed that animal companions represented a sure sign of a witch. These animals were known as "familiars" and were believed to have come from the devil himself. Cats were the most common familiars, but a range of animals—toads, owls, hedgehogs, crows, rabbits, and even hogs—were considered possible familiars for witches.

According to legend, these animals provided not only companionship, but valuable ingredients for spells. Many believed that toad's spittle, for example, was a key ingredient in a potion that supposedly made a person invisible. They also believed that in return for an animal's help, the witch would reward the familiars with a few drops of blood, which the animal would allegedly suck from a magical nipple called a witch's teat.

Women who were accused of witchcraft were thoroughly examined for any growths on their bodies that could be used for suckling familiars. Whenever a woman was convicted of witchcraft, her familiars—especially cats—were burned alive, to make sure they could not help her escape or use magic to harm her accusers.

modern people, "Puritan belief would be an incredibly difficult religion to follow," notes Jane Kamensky, a history professor at Brandeis University, "because it's a religion of endless striving and very uncertain reward."[6]

Kamensky believes that the Puritans' inability to know whether or not they were pleasing God made them nervous and fearful. The Puritans were constantly searching for signs that would tell them whether God was pleased or angry with them. Knowing whether they were reading the situation correctly presented many challenges. As Kamensky says, a Puritan might wonder, "Does the fact that I am sitting in this particular way mean that I am predestined for hell? Maybe. Does the fact that I am pious and am doing the things that the minister tells me in church mean that . . . I am one of God's chosen people? Maybe." Kamensky comments, "How can we sense God's pleasure or displeasure? That anxiety goes right to the core."[7]

A Lifetime of Work

Puritans believed that the best way to avoid the devil was to work hard and keep the home free of anything that would waste time or cause people to be lazy. There was no question of idleness for the farm families of Salem Village. Farmwork was physically exhausting and everyone participated. Unlike those people who lived in towns, almost everything the people of Salem Village wore, every piece of furniture they used, and everything they ate, the Puritan families sewed, built, grew, or otherwise made themselves.

Puritan families were large—most had between five and 10 children—so there were plenty of laborers. By 4:30 a.m. each day, parents and children rose to do what work needed to be done. Boys helped their fathers in the fields and tended pigs, cattle, sheep, and goats. Girls spent their days with their mothers—cleaning, sewing, cooking, and taking care of younger siblings. The labor went on until after sunset.

Even the youngest members of the family were asked to work hard around the home. Samuel Sewall, a highly respected judge of the time, wrote in his diary that his daughters, aged five and seven, were expected to help by upholstering chairs in their home, as well as hand stitching curtains, pillowcases, and bedspreads.

Sundays

Religion was also time consuming for the Puritans of Salem Village. Everyone attended church every Sunday morning. The day began with a three-hour service. Following a lunch break, there was another service that lasted two hours. After that, the churchgoers went home to spend the rest of the Sabbath praying and reflecting.

Devout Puritans trudge through the snow of a New England winter to attend church. In bad weather the journey could take hours, but most went in spite of the hardship.

The allotted time for church on Sundays was not limited to five hours, however. For years there was no church in Salem Village, and villagers had to make the long trek to Salem Town every Sunday—a trip that in good weather might take between two and three hours. During the winter months when ice and snow built up on the rough roads, it could take as long as five hours.

To discourage flirtations during the service, men sat on one side of the church, while women sat on the other. During the long sermons, a churchman known as the "tithing man" walked up and down the aisles, using a long stick to poke anyone who was fidgeting or who looked drowsy or bored. The temperature in the church was stifling during the summer, and, without a stove, it was positively frigid in winter. People were allowed to bring blankets, and some even brought their dogs inside, to be used as foot warmers. In a January 1686 diary entry, Judge Samuel Sewall noted, "This day is so cold that the Sacramental Bread is frozen pretty hard, and rattles sadly as it is broken into the plates."[8]

Skipping church was not an option, however uncomfortable the weather or difficult the journey from Salem Village. Historian Frances

Hill recounts a news item from 1647 in which a man pleaded for mercy after he missed church because he was bound by the Puritan rule that forbade doing any work—including lighting a fire—on Sundays. The man had fallen into the water late on Saturday and could not light a fire the next morning to dry his only suit of clothes, and instead stayed in bed to keep warm. The man was tried and found guilty of slothfulness. His punishment was a public whipping.

Children and Puritanism

Just as they bore great responsibility for working in Salem Village, children were taught very early the tenets of their religion. Puritan parents loved their children, but they made it very clear that having fun was very low on the list of things children should do. Notes Hill, "Their diaries, letters, and sermons leave no doubt that they regarded all activities besides work and prayer as potentially sinful distractions and believed that they should be extremely wary of impulses that led to fun or amusement."[9]

For children, that meant few toys or dolls, no sporting contests or recreational games, and no dancing. Singing—unless the song being sung was a hymn—was forbidden, too. There was no school in Salem Village; if a child learned to read, it would be by way of the Bible or catechism (a brief book detailing the beliefs of the church)—two of the few books that were allowed in a Puritan home.

Parents were not being cruel; their insistence on following these rules, they believed, was for the good of their children. The church taught that all babies were born sinful, and this was seen as an inescapable and irrefutable fact of life. As Puritan minister Thomas Shepard wrote: "Every man is born stark dead in sin. He is born empty of every inward principle of life, void of all graces, and hath no more good in him (whatsoever he thinks) than a dead carrion hath. . . . Their bodies are living coffins to carry a dead soul up and down."[10]

Laboring under this view, determined parents sought to ensure that their children not anger God and diminish their chances of going to heaven. In the preface of James Janeway's widely read children's book of the seventeenth century, *A Token for Children*, Puritan minister Cotton Mather raged against the way some children behaved, warning them that by acting out they were in danger of going to hell:

> Do you dare run up and down upon the Lord's-day? Or do you keep in, to read your book, and to learn what your good parents command you? What do you say, child? Which of these two sorts are you of? . . . They which lie must go to their father, the devil, into everlasting burning; they which never pray, God will pour out his wrath upon them, and when they beg and pray in hell fire, God will not forgive them.[11]

Learning Not to Be Different

In addition to learning to fear the devil, children in Salem were also taught the importance of conforming to their community. Unlike many people in the twenty-first century who value individualism and urge their children to follow their own paths, Puritan parents stressed the need to fit in, or assimilate.

Puritans valued the group dynamic; someone speaking out against a rule or law would be chastised and his or her family suspected of encouraging such behavior. If they had any doubts, children in Salem Village needed only to pay attention to what happened to those around them who were perceived as different or who broke community rules.

Though the vast majority of Salem residents were Puritans, people of other Christian faiths also came to Salem. But one of the strictest rules in this Puritan-controlled colony was that no matter what religion someone believed in before arriving, he or she must convert to Puritanism and attend those church services regularly. In fact, nonconformity to the Puritan religion was a common failing that drew scorn and punishment.

Ironically, though freedom to worship was one of the most important reasons the Puritans immigrated to America, that freedom really applied only to the Puritans themselves. Notes Hill in her book

A Delusion of Satan, "Well-meaning folk with different beliefs were thought not misguided but evil."[12] Puritans considered it a moral duty to punish or execute people whose religious outlook did not agree with their own.

Death to Quakers

The Quakers, who began arriving in the Massachusetts Bay Colony from Europe in 1656, were frequent targets. The Puritans considered them to be dangerous intruders. As one Massachusetts court declared in 1660, the Quakers were "open enemies of government itself as established in the hands of any but men of their own principles, . . . and malignant and assiduous promoters of doctrines directly tending to subvert both our churches and state."[13]

To emphasize how serious they were about the dangers presented by Quakers, Puritan courts routinely sentenced Quakers—even Quaker women—to be whipped and hanged, simply because of their religion. Governor John Endecott of Massachusetts, a Puritan, warned Quakers that if they stayed in the colony, they must not go against any of the Puritan teachings or they would be executed. "Take heed," he told newly arrived Quakers in 1656, "ye break not our ecclesiastical laws, for then ye are sure to stretch by a halter."[14]

Nineteenth-century historian and author Horatio Rogers wrote about one Puritan minister who was quite public in his advocacy of the execution of every Quaker in the colony: "Rev. John Wilson of Massachusetts . . . said, 'I would carry fire in one hand and fagots [bundles of sticks for burning] in the other, to burn all the Quakers in the world. . . . Hang them,' he cried, 'or else'—and then he [Wilson] significantly drew his finger across his throat, suggestive of cutting it."[15]

The Need for Conformity

The Puritan insistence on conformity was not limited to religion. Puritans disapproved of anyone who broke rules or engaged in behavior that was considered odd or unseemly. Their courts considered it a crime

Public Punishments

In Puritan society, punishments for breaking rules were intended to embarrass and shame rule breakers as well as to cause them pain, says historian Frances Hill. She explains:

> Transgressors had eggs thrown at them in the pillory or the stocks, were made to stand in the marketplace with notices attached to their foreheads describing their offenses, and were publicly whipped. To read through the court records is to be overwhelmed with a sense of human vulnerability in the face of implacable authority. Page after page lists crimes such as [adultery], "railing and scolding," stealing food . . . breaking off an engagement, "unseemly speeches against the rule of the Church," and sleeping during a service and "striking him who awaked him." Almost no offense against the Puritans' rigid code of belief and behavior was too trivial for punishment.

Frances Hill, *A Delusion of Satan: The Full Story of the Salem Witch Trials.* Cambridge, MA: Da Capo, 1995, p. 10.

for someone to sing a song that was not a hymn, for example, or for a man to hug or kiss his wife in public.

Many wrongdoers were forced to serve time in the stocks, heavy wooden frames with holes that trapped a person's legs, arms, and head. Sitting or standing in the stocks for hours (and sometimes days) on end was a very public punishment. The stocks were always set up in the middle of a village or town, where passers-by could jeer and hurl insults at the accused—or even throw eggs, rotten food, or stones at them.

Puritan communities like Salem Village meted out far harsher punishments for offenses that were considered even more serious, such as expressing disapproval or criticism of government or church officials. In 1631 a man named Philip Ratcliff made comments critical of both the Massachusetts Bay Colony's government and the Salem church. For his punishment, noted one official, the court decided to "whip him, to cut off his ears, and then to banish him from the limits of civilization into a wilderness."[16]

Those who failed to conform to the rigid Puritan rules of behavior were punished. With punishments such as the stocks and pillory (pictured) members of the community publicly shamed and humiliated offenders—sometimes for hours on end.

People were not only punished for breaking laws, but also for acting differently from what was considered the norm. For example, since most adults married, Puritans viewed those who stayed single with suspicion—especially women. So too were people suspect who had birthmarks, who hummed or sang while they worked, or who occasionally talked to themselves. Puritans believed that such actions could be signs that such people were under the spell of a witch's charm, or that they might themselves be witches.

Babies born with physical handicaps were called "monsters" or "demons." Puritans believed that such babies were the product of a sexual union between a woman and the devil. In some cases the court ordered the execution of the mother of such a child, as well as the midwife who assisted at the birth. One Massachusetts village permanently banished a young woman who delivered a stillborn baby that was deformed. The community believed that the baby's deformities were a sign that God was displeased with the mother—and that the village would suffer if it did not take action.

Dealing with Witches

The presence of witches within a community was seen as one of the surest signs that God was displeased with the people of that community. Because they had brought many of their superstitions and fears about witchcraft from England, the Puritans considered themselves supremely knowledgeable about witches. For instance, they *knew* with absolute certainty that witches rode on poles and did most of their evil work during the nighttime hours.

Though witches could be either male or female, most of those identified as witches were older women. They tended to be solitary, except for their animal companions (known as familiars), who often assisted them in their sinister work. Because it was believed that witches had close bonds with particular animals, anyone who seemed friendly with an animal—even giving a dog or horse a name—was viewed with suspicion in Puritan communities.

The Puritans also believed that anyone suspected of witchcraft must be quickly arrested, tried, and executed to prevent the wrath of an angry God. Thus, when signs of witches in their midst arose in 1692, the Puritans of Salem Village could not control the storm that engulfed them. That storm, writes Salem researcher Robert Rapley, swept everything before it, more like a tornado in its effect, "tossing lives into turmoil, spreading fear, and hatred, and death, leaving nobody unterrified or untouched."[17]

Chapter 2

Murmurs and Accusations

Salem Village began experiencing its first threat of witchcraft in 1692. However, in the years just before, there were a few other occurrences of alleged witchcraft in other places within New England. Though none of these was on the same massive, hysteria-producing scale as the outbreaks in Europe, they certainly fed the Puritans' unease and fear.

In 1655 a Boston widow named Anne Hibbins was accused of being a witch. Hibbins had a reputation of being quarrelsome and generally difficult to get along with. Her accusers were two women who had been gossiping about her. Though she was too far away to hear their words, Hibbins said she knew that the women were talking about her. The women were convinced that she must have supernatural powers in order to know about their private conversation. Hibbins was formally charged with witchcraft.

At her trial the jury found her guilty, but the judges in the case were reluctant to accept the verdict handed down by the jury. Instead, they sent the case to a higher court, which eventually concurred with the previous jury and found Hibbins guilty. The governor of the colony sentenced her to death and she was hanged in 1656.

The Case of Goody Glover

In 1688, just four years before the witch trials began in Salem, another Boston woman was accused of witchcraft. The children of a stonemason named John Goodwin began to exhibit disturbing behaviors.

Thirteen-year-old Martha, the oldest of the children, had recently questioned the family's laundress, thinking that she may have stolen some linen. The laundress's mother, Goodwife Glover (married women of the lower classes were not called "Mrs." but rather "Goodwife," often shortened to "Goody"), sharply scolded Martha for having the nerve to accuse her daughter of theft.

Soon after that confrontation, Martha, her two sisters, and one of her brothers began to suffer a number of strange symptoms. According to respected Puritan minister Cotton Mather, sometimes the children

> would be deaf, sometimes dumb, and sometimes blind, and often, all this at once. One while [time] their tongues would be drawn down their throats; another while they would be pulled out upon their chins, to a prodigious length. They would have their mouths opened unto such a wideness, that their jaws went out of joint; and anon [soon] they would clap together again with a force like that of a strong spring-lock. The same would happen to their shoulder-blades, and their elbows and hand-wrists, and several of their joints. . . . They would make the most piteous of outcries, that they were cut with knives, and struck with blows that they could not bear. Their necks would be broken, so that their neck-bone would seem dissolved unto them that felt after it; and yet on the sudden, it would become again so stiff that there was no stirring of their heads; yea, their heads would be twisted almost round.[18]

Glover was arrested and charged with witchcraft. At her trial, Mather testified that she was "a scandalous old Irishwoman, very poor, a Roman [Catholic] and obstinate in idolatry."[19] She was quickly found guilty and sentenced to hang. Some historians say that Glover's fate was sealed with the Puritans simply because she was Catholic.

Four years before the start of the Salem witch trials, the Puritan minister Cotton Mather testified against a Boston woman who was charged with witchcraft. Here, Mather kneels in prayer in an effort to save a woman thought to be a victim of witchcraft.

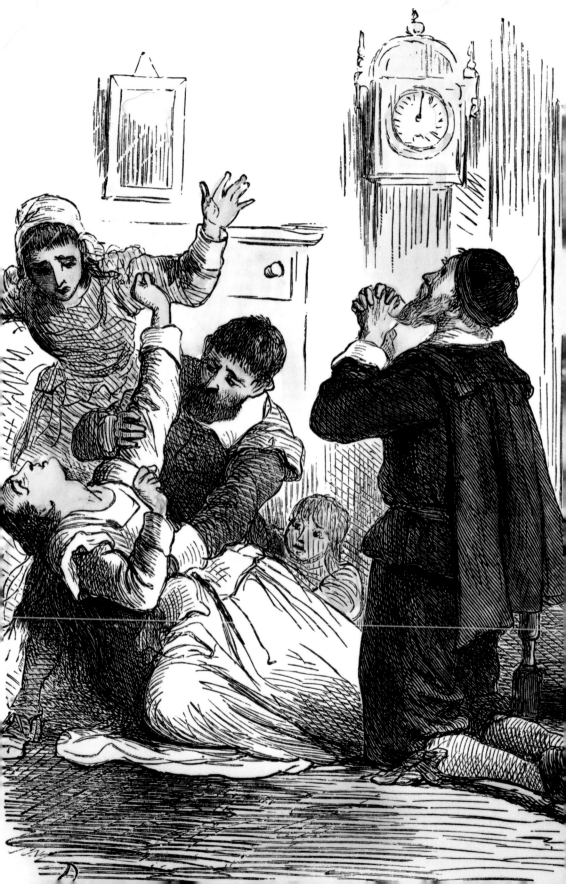

Doubts of the Chosen People

Such cases as these were often talked about in Salem Village. In fact, say historians, it is very likely that some of the people in Salem Village might have made the journey to Boston to witness the hanging of Glover. Puritans enjoyed watching hangings, and rather than shielding their children from witnessing something so unpleasant, they often encouraged their children to watch. Many Puritan parents believed that watching people being executed for crimes against God was a good way to teach children of all ages what happens to those who follow devilish impulses.

But while it was gratifying to see witches executed, there was usually a sense of concern, too. Many Puritans were convinced that such episodes of witchcraft were signs that God might no longer consider the Puritans his chosen people. These incidents were fairly rare, but even so, anytime villagers heard of someone suspected of dabbling in witchcraft or acting suspiciously, it made them worry all the more.

In 1692 reports of witchcraft virtually exploded in Salem Village. Not surprisingly, when the rumors spread that some in their village were practicing witchcraft, people were horrified. But what was even more bewildering was the alleged source of the witchcraft—the home of their minister, the Reverend Samuel Parris.

In the Minister's House

Parris and his family had moved to Salem Village in 1689, just three years before. His household consisted of his wife, Elizabeth; three children; his orphaned niece Abigail; and two West Indian slaves—Tituba and her husband John Indian. Nine-year-old Betty and 11-year-old Abigail spent a great deal of time together. Because Elizabeth was often unwell, the two young girls were frequently left in the care of Tituba.

The girls enjoyed hearing Tituba's stories of her childhood in Barbados. They especially loved her accounts of black magic, ghosts, and voodoo that she witnessed as a young girl. Evil spirits were fea-

Swimming a Witch

A frequently used method for proving the guilt or innocence of witches was called "swimming," or sometimes "ducking." The accused witch was bound by the right thumb to the left big toe, and the left thumb to the right big toe. Afterward, the victim was plunged into a river or lake to see if he or she would sink or float. It was believed that a witch would float, while an innocent person would sink. The method was used as long ago as the seventeenth century BC in Babylonia and as recently as 1706 in the American colony of Virginia. Because suspected witches were bound so that they could neither swim nor tread water, victims of this ordeal usually drowned. In essence, whether or not they were guilty hardly mattered.

tured prominently in these stories—something that must have been both exciting and scary for Betty and Abigail, since the fear of the devil was so great among the Puritans. The girls certainly knew that Betty's father would be very angry if he knew what they were doing. According to historians William J. Birnes and Joel Martin, Tituba must have told the stories "with such an intensity that the children found them exciting, perhaps all the more so because they were forbidden."[20]

Perhaps spurred on by Tituba's stories, the girls began playing games that were said to predict the future. One such game was breaking an egg and slipping the white into a glass of water. The shape of the white was thought to give the person a clue as to his or her destiny. Once, when Betty and Abigail were playing this game, the egg white took the shape of a coffin, frightening them. John Hale, a pastor in nearby Beverly, later wrote that he was well acquainted with the case and had been told that one of the girls "did try with an egg and a glass to find her future husband's calling; till there came up a coffin, that is a spectre in likeness of a coffin."[21]

Most of the time, however, the fortune-telling games were fun. Historians believe that Betty and Abigail told some of their friends about Tituba's stories and charms. These friends—ranging in age from 12 to 18—apparently began visiting the Parris home to partake in fortune-telling and other forbidden activities.

Strange Behavior

In January 1692 Betty and Abigail began displaying odd behaviors. The girls stared off into space while they were supposed to be reading, praying, or sewing. Robert Calef, a critic of clergy during the witch trials, writes in his 1700 book, *More Wonders of the Invisible World*, that the girls' behavior became even more erratic. "They began to act in a strange and unusual manner," he writes, "by getting into holes and creeping under chairs and stools, and to use sundry odd postures and antic gestures, uttering foolish, ridiculous speeches, which neither they themselves, nor any others could make sense of."[22]

Such actions were both frightening and worrisome to Parris and his wife, and they were not sure what to do. Doctors were unable to find a physical cause for their odd behavior. Parris urged the girls to fast and pray, hoping that these things might help them return to health. Neither helped, however; in fact, their odd behavior became more frequent and more public. Both Betty and Abigail began having fits in church and outside their home—in full view of astonished villagers. It was not long before people began to talk about sorcery and suggest that the girls had fallen under the spell of an evil witch.

Villagers stopped by the Parris house, hoping to see for themselves what was going on with Betty and Abigail. Hale visited from Beverly, and he agreed with doctors who suspected something other than sickness or disease:

These children were bitten and pinched by invisible agents. Their arms, necks, and backs turned this way and that way, and returned back again, so as it was impossible for them to do of themselves, and beyond the power of any epileptic fits, or natural disease to effect. Sometimes they were taken dumb, their mouths stopped, their throats choked, their limbs wracked and tormented so as might move an heart of stone, to sympathize with them, with bowels of compassion for them.[23]

"Under an Evil Hand"

Parris's predecessor at the Salem Village church, the Reverend Deodat Lawson, also dropped in at the Parris home in early March 1692 after hearing about the bizarre behavior of the two girls. Lawson later testified in court that he witnessed Abigail's odd behavior firsthand while talking with Parris:

> I went to give Mr. Parris a visit. When I was there, his kinswoman, Abigail Williams, (about 12 years of age) had a grievous fit; she was at first hurried with violence to and fro in the room . . . sometimes making as if she would fly, stretching her arms up as high as she could, and crying "whish, whish, whish!" several times. . . . After that, she run to the fire, and began to throw fire brands about the house; and run against the back, as if she would run up the chimney, and as they said, she had attempted to go into the fire in other fits.[24]

Historians say that Parris must have been aware of the rumors that his daughter and niece were under some sort of malicious spell. He might even have suspected it himself. Like other Puritan ministers of that time, Parris feared the devil and his agents of evil, such as witches and sorcerers. The devil and his agents were very real to him, and one only needed to read the Bible to verify their existence.

Puritan parents encouraged their children to watch public hangings. Such sights were thought to provide a valuable lesson to young people who might be tempted to test society's rules.

In the book of Exodus, for example, people are warned, "Thou shalt not suffer [allow] a witch to live."[25] In the New Testament a verse from the first book of Peter warns, "Be sober, be vigilant, because thy adversary the devil, as a roaring lion, walketh about, whom he may devour."[26] For devout Puritans such as Parris and his congregation, these biblical verses were not merely symbolic, but something to be taken literally.

It was difficult for Parris to admit that his daughter and niece could be in league with the devil under his own roof. But when William Griggs, a local physician, bluntly told him that it seemed clear that the girls were "under an Evil hand,"[27] Parris was forced to agree that the diagnosis made sense. But the question remained: What was to be done?

The Witch Cake

If the girls were indeed under the spell of a witch, it was crucial to find out the identity of the witch. Villagers asked Betty and Abigail who had bewitched them, but the girls said nothing. By late February 1692, with the girls still acting strangely and with no clue as to who was responsible, a neighbor named Mary Sibley decided to take matters into her own hands. Without consulting either Parris or his wife, she directed the Parris's servants, Tituba and Indian, to bake a witch cake.

A witch cake, well known to English people in those days, was a cake baked from cornmeal or rye flour mixed with urine from the person or persons suspected of being under the spell of witchcraft. The cake would then be fed to an animal—often the family dog. If the person was truly the victim of a witch's spell, people believed, the witch

cake would make the animal act strangely, too—thereby confirming the diagnosis. If the Parris family dog had a reaction to eating the witch cake ordered by Sibley, those records have not survived.

"The Devil Hath Been Raised Amongst Us"

When Parris learned about Sibley's actions, he was both angry and fearful, says Salem witch trial expert Frances Hill, who has studied Parris's journals, sermons, and other writings. Hill writes:

> He must have sensed that [the witch cake] could only make matters even worse than they were. To come across what seemed an ordinary cake, made of cornmeal, and find it contained his relatives' urine, for devilish purposes, at a time when the family was already in uproar, the young people in fits, his wife beside herself and perhaps blaming him, must have deepened his terrible dread of events running out of control, and damning them all, both in this world and the next.[28]

Parris was also furious with Tituba and Indian for their part in the witch cake episode. However, most of his fury was aimed at Sibley. He scolded her, not only for interfering, but because she chose to use devilish means to resolve the situation. In Parris's view, Sibley's actions endangered not only Betty and Abigail but also the entire village. He even chastised Sibley from the pulpit for what he described as "going to the Devil for help against the Devil." Parris said in his sermon:

> Diabolical means was used, by the making of a cake by my Indian man, who had his direction from this our sister Mary Sibley: since which [time] apparitions have been plenty, and exceeding much mischief hath followed. But by this means (it seems) the Devil hath been raised amongst us, and his rage is vehement and terrible, and when he shall be silenced the Lord only knows.[29]

Possessed?

In her book *The Devil in Massachusetts,* historian Marion Lena Starkey describes the bizarre behavior of nine-year-old Betty Parris, once known to her family and friends as a docile, even-tempered, well-behaved child.

> Sometimes her mother found her sitting all alone at her needlework, her hands poised but motionless, her eyes staring with uncanny fixity at an invisible object. "Betty," her mother would say, and the child would start violently as if caught in an act of guilt, scream sharply, and being pressed for an explanation would give utterance to a meaningless babbling.
>
> It came on even in prayer, in fact after a while particularly in prayer. When all heads were supposedly bowed, [Reverend Samuel] Parris would steal a sidelong glance of inspection and discover that Betty had remained upright, her eyes fixed in that deathlike stare. Better, he soon learned, to leave her be, for if he reproved her, she remained rigid as ever, but worked her mouth and gave off curious hoarse choking sounds, sometimes almost like the barking of a dog.

Marion Lena Starkey, *The Devil in Massachusetts: A Modern Enquiry Into the Salem Witch Trials.* New York: Doubleday, 1969, pp. 39–40.

Parris did not believe Sibley acted out of meanness. "What she did, she did it ignorantly, from what she had heard of this nature from other ignorant, or worse, persons,"[30] he said in the same sermon. He ended by calling for a show of hands from the congregation on whether Sibley should be forgiven. The vote was unanimous in favor of forgiveness.

The First Accusations

As the problems in Salem Village were multiplying others in the village—some of them friends of Betty and Abigail—began acting strangely, too. Ann Putnam, the 12-year-old daughter of influential farmer Thomas Putnam, began to show the same symptoms—writhing, shrieking, barking, and screaming for no apparent reason. So did 17-year-old Elizabeth Hubbard, the niece of Griggs, who had suggested to Parris that Betty and Abigail were victims of witchcraft. Over the next few weeks, several others would show the signs and symptoms of bewitchment.

Pressed for an explanation of their behavior, Betty, Abigail, Ann, and Elizabeth (who later became known collectively as "the afflicted girls") named three women whom they blamed for bewitching them. The first was the Parris family slave Tituba—because of her involvement in the fortune-telling and scary storytelling. They claimed that Tituba could make herself invisible and then inflict pain on them, which meant that no one could witness her actions. According to statements the girls gave to magistrates in Salem, Tituba "did pinch, prick, and grievously torment them, and that they saw her here and there, where nobody else could. Yea, they could tell where she was, and what she did, when out of their human sight."[31]

Another woman named by the girls was Sarah Good, a pregnant, middle-aged woman of Salem Village. Good's story was tragic—her father, a wealthy innkeeper, had disgraced the family by committing suicide when she was 19. Her stepfather had cheated her out of her inheritance, and she had been poor ever since. Her husband, William, was in jail for not paying his debts, and as a result, Sarah survived by begging for herself and her children. She was an odd, eccentric woman, with flyaway, prematurely gray hair. She talked and grumbled to herself and habitually smoked a pipe. Because of her diminished status in the community, people were not at all surprised when the girls named her as a witch. In his book *Wayward Puritans: A Study in the Sociology of Deviance*, sociologist Kai T. Erikson describes her as "a proper hag of a witch if Salem village had ever seen one."[32]

The third woman was Sarah Osborne, age 69, another whom Salem villagers looked down on. After the 1674 death of her husband, Robert Prince, she purchased an indentured servant, Alexander Osborne, for the sum of 15 pounds, which was a great deal of money in those days. What horrified the villagers was that she and Alexander lived as husband and wife without being married. Though the two later married, the damage to her reputation had been done. Sarah had stopped attending church recently—another offense that shocked the Puritan villagers. Any woman who did not attend church on Sundays was clearly not a Christian woman, they believed, and it would not be surprising if she were guilty of witchcraft.

An Overflow Crowd

As townspeople began panicking about what seemed to be the spreading influence of the devil in Salem Village, four well-respected men of the community took action. Thomas Putnam, his brother Edward Putnam, Joseph Hutchinson, and Thomas Preston appeared before Salem magistrates. On February 29, 1692, they filed official complaints of witchcraft against Tituba, Sarah Good, and Sarah Osborne. The three women were arrested and jailed. They were required to appear at a hearing the following day, during which Salem Town magistrates would decide whether there was enough evidence against the women to proceed with a formal trial.

The plan was to hold these preliminary hearings in Samuel Ingersoll's tavern in Salem Village. However, by the time the three prisoners arrived at the tavern, the crowd had swollen in size, and it was clear that the tavern would be too small a venue. Evidently, no farming, lessons, or housework were being done that day, for it seemed that every man, woman, and child was standing at the side of the road watching the arrival of the accused witches.

Realizing the need for more space, the magistrates transferred the event to the meetinghouse, where church services were usually held. Spectators hurried into the meetinghouse and squeezed onto the benches, hoping for a good view. The prisoners waited outside for their turn to be examined by the magistrates. When Parris walked to the pulpit to offer a prayer, everything was silent. Then word was sent to the constables to send in the first prisoner. After that moment, nothing would ever be the same in Salem Village.

Chapter 3

The Hearings Begin

I n the modern US judicial system, a person charged with a crime is presumed innocent until proven guilty. The accused is also guaranteed a lawyer, even if he or she cannot afford one, and the lawyer questions the witnesses before a judge or jury. This was not the case in seventeenth-century Salem Village. The magistrates, or judges, directly questioned the accused, who had no one to advise or speak for them. The trial took place in stages, beginning with a magistrate's hearing. In this first hearing before the trial began, the magistrates were officials from Salem Town, John Hathorne and Jonathan Corwin.

Sarah Good's Hearing

Their first interview was with Sarah Good. Hardly a model prisoner, Good had tried three times to escape by leaping from her horse while being escorted from the jail to the site of the hearing. Historians say that during her hearing, Good was rude and confrontational—neither of which helped her case. The clerk at her hearing, Ezekiel Cheever, later noted that Good's responses to the magistrates' questions were delivered "in a very wicked, spiteful manner, reflecting and retorting against the authority with base and abusive words."[33]

While the magistrates were supposed to examine the prisoners in a neutral manner, it was evident from the beginning of Hathorne's questioning of Good that he was convinced of her guilt. Onlookers in the packed meetinghouse were still, hanging on every word. The following is the first exchange between Hathorne and Good:

"Sarah Good, what evil spirit have you familiarity with?"

"None."

"Have you made no contract with the devil?"

"No."

"Why do you hurt these children?"

"I do not hurt them. I scorn it [witchcraft]."

"Who do you employ then to do it?"

"I employ nobody."

"What creature do you employ then?"

"No creature, but I am falsely accused."[34]

As Good continued to deny that she had bewitched the girls, Hathorne turned to the victims, Betty Parris and Abigail Williams, and asked them if Good was the woman who had tormented them. They answered "yes," and immediately began moaning and convulsing, writhing as though in great pain. Hathorne took this as a sign that Good was lying. He then asked: "Sarah Good, do you not see now what you have done? Why do you not tell us the truth? Why do you thus torment these poor children?"[35]

Her answer—that she did not torment them and that she was telling the truth—seemed preposterous in the face of the moaning and writhing of the young girls. Predictably, the onlookers were convinced of Good's guilt, as were the magistrates, and she was quickly returned to jail.

Sarah Osborne

The next prisoner to be examined was Sarah Osborne, and she fared no better. Weak and clearly not feeling well, she repeatedly denied being a witch. When the magistrates asked the girls whether Osborne was the one who had bewitched them, they all said "yes" and began having fits again, just as they had with Sarah Good.

Osborne insisted that she was more likely to be under a witch's spell than to be a witch herself. She told the magistrates that she had once been frightened by a vision in her sleep and either saw or

Deodat Lawson's Testimony

The minister Deodat Lawson testified during one of the early examinations about whether the fits the afflicted girls displayed seemed faked or real. In this part of his testimony, quoted by Frances Hill in *A Delusion of Satan,* Lawson insists that what he witnessed could not have been an act.

> Sometimes, in their fits, they have had their tongues drawn out of their mouths to a fearful length, their heads turned very much over their shoulders; and while they have been so strained in their fits, and had their arms and legs, etc., wrested as if they were quite dislocated, the blood hath gushed plentifully out of their mouths for a considerable time together, which some, that they might be satisfied that it was real blood, took upon their finger, and rubbed on their other hand. I saw several together thus violently strained and bleeding in their fits, to my very great astonishment that my fellow-mortals should be so grievously distressed by the invisible powers of darkness. For certainly all considerate persons who beheld these things must needs be convinced, that their motions in their fits were preternatural and involuntary, both as to the manner, which was so strange as a well person could not (at least without great pain) screw their bodies into.

Quoted in Frances Hill, *A Delusion of Satan: The Full Story of the Salem Witch Trials.* Cambridge, MA: Da Capo, 1995, pp. 44–45.

dreamed "a thing like an Indian, all black, which did pinch her in the neck and pulled her by the back part of her head to the door of the house."[36]

Osborne's attempt to paint herself as a victim rather than a perpetrator did not help her cause. The most damning bit of evidence against Osborne, besides the afflicted girls' fits, was the fact that she had not been regular in her church attendance. Like Good, Osborne returned to her jail cell to await a formal trial.

Tituba's Confession

If the villagers who crowded into the meetinghouse expected the third hearing to be similar to those of Good and Osborne, they were greatly mistaken. The examination started predictably enough, with Hathorne asking Tituba if she had frightened and hurt the girls, which she denied. He also asked her if she had any familiarity with the devil or evil spirits, and she answered that she did not.

Under Hathorne's relentless questions about Tituba's relationship with the devil, she eventually changed her testimony. She admitted to having personal contact with Satan. "The Devil," Tituba said to Hathorne, "came to me and bid me serve him."[37]

As the questioning continued, Tituba stated that the devil had threatened to kill the children and to kill her if she did not do his bidding. She described him as a man wearing "black clothes sometimes, sometimes [a] serge coat of other color,"[38] and that he appeared sometimes as a black dog and once as a hog.

Naming Names

The spectators were enthralled by Tituba's responses to Hathorne's questions. The afflicted girls, who had been convulsing, wailing, and moaning as they had been during the previous examinations of Good and Osborne, suddenly stilled. As historian Marion Lena Starkey notes, the girls "became quiet as so many sleeping babes . . . hanging with rapt attention on Tituba's every word."[39]

Tituba, a slave from Barbados, entertains children with stories of black magic, ghosts, and voodoo. Her stories led to charges of witchcraft and a confession of contact with the devil.

Tituba described the book that the devil carried with him. She said it listed nine of his followers, including Good and Osborne. She described the familiars, animal helpers believed to be provided to witches by the devil. She said that Good had a yellow bird that attended her, and Osborne had "a thing with a head like a woman, with two legs and wings."[40] Tituba also described how she flew with Osborne and Good on a pole or stick to do their witchcraft. "We ride taking hold of one another," she told Hathorne. "[I] don't know how we go, for I saw no trees nor path, but was presently there."[41]

Over the next five days, the women were examined again by magistrates, who agreed that there was enough evidence against Good, Osborne, and Tituba for them to stand trial for witchcraft. They were taken to Boston's jail to await their trials. But while having them in jail may have been somewhat comforting to villagers, the hearings had been unsettling. According to Tituba, the devil had a book with nine witches listed. With Good, Osborne, and Tituba in jail, that left at least six more unaccounted for. Who, Salem's citizens wondered, were the other witches in their midst?

"A Gospel Woman"

It did not take long for the girls to accuse another woman. It happened on March 11, a proclaimed day of fasting and prayer in Salem Village, when ministers from the area visited the Parris home to pray for the afflicted girls. During prayers, Ann Putnam began screaming that Martha Corey was a witch who was tormenting her.

The name was a surprise. The 65-year-old woman was well liked in the community. She was a regular churchgoer who in her own words was "a gospel woman."[42] Historians say that her attitude toward the witch hearings may well have made her a target of negative attention. Corey did not believe the afflicted girls, and she said so—not only to her family, but to others in the community. She did not attend the hearings and tried to talk her husband out of going, too.

Corey was arrested soon after being named, and she appeared before the magistrates. As had happened in previous hearings, the girls writhed and screamed when she walked in, as though she were torturing them. Ann claimed she had seen Corey with a familiar—a yellow bird—which Corey was feeding with the skin between her fingers.

During the hearing, Ann and the other girls continued their fits as Corey stood before the magistrates. According to one account, Corey "bit her lip, likely from the stress and fright of her predicament. At the exact same time, the girls loudly screamed that they were being nipped. As Corey held her hands so her fingers tightened, no doubt from nervousness, the girls hollered in pain."[43]

Such evidence was more than enough for the magistrates, who sent her to jail. As she walked from the meetinghouse, Corey insisted that no matter how hard they tried, they could never prove that she was a witch. However, writes Starkey, "such a statement was beside the point. What she couldn't prove, what no one at all accused of such a thing could prove, was that she wasn't."[44]

More Accusations

The accusation against Corey was followed by a flood of others. Rebecca Nurse, like Corey, considered the hearings foolish. She was a well-liked 71-year-old woman who loved spending her days caring for her grandchildren. When she was confronted by officials who announced that she had been accused, she was flabbergasted and expressed worry that her accusers were going too far. "I am troubled, oh I am troubled

In the popular imagination, witches fly on brooms and often are accompanied by familiars—cats or other animals provided by the devil. In the witchcraft trial of Martha Corey, one young accuser claimed to have seen Corey with a familiar—a yellow bird.

at some of [the afflicted girls'] crying out," she said. "Some of the persons they have spoken of are, as I believe, as innocent as I."[45]

The first to claim to have seen Nurse's specter, or ghost, was 12-year-old Ann Putnam. The encounter, she claimed, caused her to have fits and convulsions. A few days later, her mother—Ann Putnam—also claimed to have seen Nurse's apparition. She told officials that she was resting in bed "after being wearied out in helping to tend my poor afflicted child," when all of a sudden she felt "almost pressed and choked to death"[46] by Nurse's specter.

Over the next few days, Ann's mother claimed, she saw the specter again and again. One time, she said, Nurse "appeared to me only in her shift [nightgown] and brought a little red book . . . urging me vehemently to write [in it]." Because she refused to write in the book, Putnam said, "she threatened to tear my soul out of my body."[47] Because of the Putnams' allegations, officials arrested Nurse and scheduled her hearing for March 24.

No Tears

For the first time since the hearings began, the magistrates were sympathetic to someone accused of witchcraft. Nurse was hard of hearing and clearly bewildered by the charges. She seemed confused as to why anyone would say such things about her—especially since she had been sick in bed for more than a week. "I am innocent and clear," she said, "and have not been able to get out of doors. . . . I never afflicted no child, no, never in my life."[48]

As Nurse stood in front of the magistrates and crowds of spectators, the afflicted girls began their seizures and moaning. When Nurse spread her hands in helplessness, the girls spread theirs, and from then on they imitated every one of Nurse's movements. It looked to spectators and the magistrates as though the girls were under Nurse's control.

Though sympathetic toward Nurse in the beginning, Hathorne changed his view. The reason for this change, it soon became clear, was that Nurse had not cried when facing her accusers and answering the questions of the magistrates. Witches, people believed, could not shed tears. At one point in the hearing, Hathorne observed, "It is very awful to all to see these agonies and you, [a church member] thus charged with contracting with the Devil . . . and yet to stand with dry eyes, when there are so many wet."[49] Like all the women examined before her, Nurse was sent to jail in Boston to await a formal trial.

A Turning Point

Nurse's hearing was a turning point for Salem Village. Many people in the village were stunned that Nurse, a churchgoing woman who was such a beloved member of the community, could be a witch. After all, Samuel Parris had told them in a recent sermon that as members of Christ's church they were guaranteed, in historian Bryan Le Beau's words, "safe passage by God over troubled seas, secure at least within its doors from the corrupting influence of the Devil."[50] If Nurse and Corey were in league with the devil, they worried, what did that say about their church? With witches in the congregation, how could they ever feel safe again?

Parris provided the answer the following Sunday, on March 27, 1692, in another sermon. He reminded them that even among Jesus's disciples, there was a traitor—Judas. Therefore, Parris said, the church must be composed of both good and evil. "Let none . . . build their hopes of salvation merely upon this, that they are church members. This you and I may be," he told them, "and yet devils for all that."[51]

With such words, Parris had opened the door to a flurry of new accusations.

"From that time on," notes witch trial historian Robert Rapley, "accusations could be made against anybody, no matter how good they appeared to be in moral or religious life. Within this community, with [Parris's] advice and blessing, any accusation could be valid."[52]

Opening the Floodgates

Following Parris's sermon, witchcraft accusations sharply increased. It seemed that each day brought more charges. Many of these charges were against people who either did not believe in witches or who doubted the authenticity of the afflicted girls' claims.

One of the saddest cases was that of Dorcas Good, the daughter of the alleged witch Sarah Good. At age four, she was the youngest person accused during the Salem witch hunts. Dorcas's accusers, as in the case of all the others, were the afflicted girls. They claimed that Dorcas had been running around the countryside, biting them, as historian Marion Starkey notes, "like a little mad dog."[53] If her mother had not already been sent to jail by the magistrates, Dorcas might not have been a suspect. But during the little girl's hearing, two of the afflicted girls began their screaming and convulsing when Dorcas looked at them. They also showed bite marks on their arms that they claimed had been left by Dorcas.

Most convincing was the conversation Dorcas had with John Higginson, the minister of Salem Town, before her hearing began. Higginson claimed later that she told him she had a little snake as a pet. Higginson took that to mean that Dorcas had, as many witches allegedly did, a familiar—evidence that was as damning in the eyes of the spectators and magistrates as the bite marks on the afflicted girls' arms. Dorcas was sent to jail in Boston, to be with her mother until her trial.

Naysayers and Disbelievers

One case in the flood of new accusations was that of John Proctor, who was fed up with the trials—especially because he did not believe that the girls were really bewitched. Mary Warren, who had joined the ranks of the afflicted girls, worked as a servant in Proctor's home. Soon after Nurse's hearing, Proctor stormed into the village and demanded to take her home where she belonged. He scoffed at the idea that she was under any spell and insisted that the foolish accusations had gotten out of hand. If the girls were left to continue their rants, he said, "we should all be devils and witches quickly."[54] His idea was that if the girls received a good whipping, they would soon stop their accusations. Predictably, the girls quickly claimed to see the specters

A Hathorne Descendant's Shame

The Hathorne name was well known and well respected in Puritan society. William Hathorne was a strict Puritan who had Quakers whipped in the streets of Salem. His son, John Hathorne, served as one of the most aggressive of the witch trial magistrates.

One of the most famous American novelists and short story writers of the 1800s, Nathaniel Hawthorne, was a direct descendant of William and John. Born in Salem, Massachusetts, 112 years after the witch trials, Nathaniel's surname at birth was also Hathorne. But when he reached adulthood he was so ashamed of his ancestors that he decided to add a "w" to the spelling of his surname to set himself apart.

In the introduction to his most famous novel, *The Scarlet Letter*, Hawthorne writes that he is haunted by the actions of John and William Hathorne and that he has no idea whether his ancestors ever regretted their actions. For that reason, Hawthorne writes, "I, the present writer, as their representative, hereby take shame upon myself for their sakes."

Quoted in Nathaniel Hawthorne, *The Scarlet Letter*. New York: Bantam, 1981, p. 9.

of both Proctor and his wife Elizabeth. The two were also sent to jail to await trial.

Another who scorned the witchcraft charges was Nurse's sister, Sarah Cloyse. Soon after Nurse's hearing, Cloyse attended a Sunday church service. When Parris began his sermon, which dealt with Jesus asking which of his disciples was actually a devil, Cloyse was furious. Feeling that Parris was making a comment about her sister's guilt, she stormed from the church, slamming the door behind her. It was not long before the afflicted girls claimed they saw Cloyse's specter drinking blood with others accused of witchcraft, and she was soon jailed.

Surprising Specters

With the unexpected outpouring of accusations from the afflicted girls, the two magistrates in Salem could not keep up. Five esteemed officials from Boston joined Hathorne and Corwin as magistrates on April 11, 1692. The addition of new magistrates helped make the examination of so many accused citizens move along more quickly.

It was good timing, for during the next week, four more warrants were issued.

One of the most surprising arrests was that of Mary Warren, the afflicted girl who had worked for the Proctors. Soon after Proctor and his wife had been examined and sent to jail, Mary began recanting her earlier testimony about people she had accused. She also suggested that the other afflicted girls had lied during their testimonies. Almost immediately, the other afflicted girls turned on her and accused her of writing in the devil's book. After her hearing, she was sent to jail but was later released when she began having fits again. She subsequently rejoined the afflicted girls.

Another surprising arrest was that of George Burroughs, who had been a minister in Salem Village years before. He had not been especially well liked, and he remained at the church for only two years. His tenure there had been a sad one, for his second wife had died during his time in Salem Village. When Ann Putnam, one of the afflicted girls, named Burroughs, she said that his specter was haunting her, telling her that he had killed two of his wives by bewitching them.

That seemed reason enough for marshals to ride to Maine (then part of Massachusetts) to bring Burroughs back for a hearing. As with almost all those brought before the magistrates, Burroughs was detained until a formal trial could be held. He and the other prisoners were chained together and placed in a wooden cart for delivery to the jail.

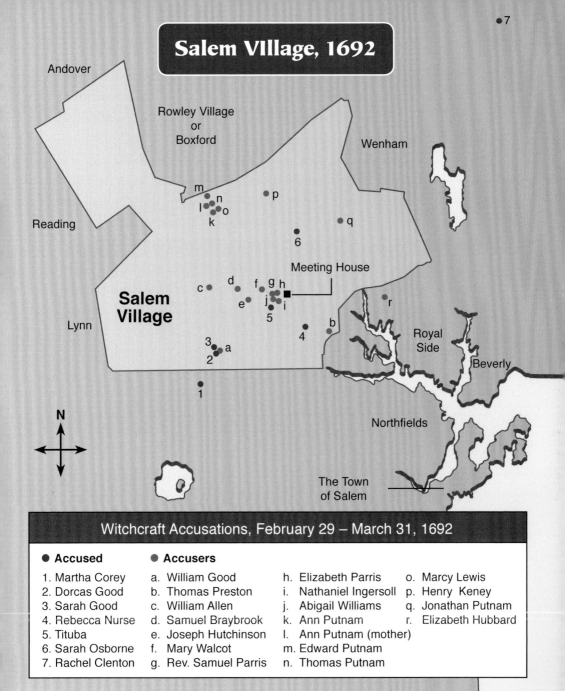

Salem VIllage, 1692

Andover

Rowley Village
or
Boxford

Wenham

Reading

m
n
l
o
k
p
q

6

Meeting House

Salem
Village

c
d
f g h
e
j
i
5

r

Lynn

Royal
Side

4

b

3
a
2

Beverly

1

N

Northfields

The Town
of Salem

Witchcraft Accusations, February 29 – March 31, 1692

● **Accused**   ● **Accusers**

1. Martha Corey
2. Dorcas Good
3. Sarah Good
4. Rebecca Nurse
5. Tituba
6. Sarah Osborne
7. Rachel Clenton

a. William Good
b. Thomas Preston
c. William Allen
d. Samuel Braybrook
e. Joseph Hutchinson
f. Mary Walcot
g. Rev. Samuel Parris

h. Elizabeth Parris
i. Nathaniel Ingersoll
j. Abigail Williams
k. Ann Putnam
l. Ann Putnam (mother)
m. Edward Putnam
n. Thomas Putnam

o. Marcy Lewis
p. Henry Keney
q. Jonathan Putnam
r. Elizabeth Hubbard

A Place of Horrors

Because of the flood of people being accused, jail space was at a premium. The jail in Salem Town was full, and the jails in Boston and Ipswich soon overflowed, too. The prisoners were held in deplorable conditions; the jails were foul smelling with the stink of unwashed bodies, human waste, and disease. Prisoners were denied even basic medical care. Sarah Osborne, who had been ill at the time of her hearing, died in her prison cell.

Accused witches were treated worse than other prisoners. To keep their specters from escaping, they were shackled in chains that were bolted to the wall. They could not lie down, and they had no toilet facilities other than the thin layer of straw spread over the stone floors. The cells were cold in the winter and hot and smelly in the summer.

As the already overcrowded jails filled with more and more accused witches, the prisoners must have wondered how things could have become so terrible so quickly. But if any of these wretched inmates imagined a brighter future once the formal trials began, they were sadly mistaken.

Chapter 4

Trials and Punishments

In mid-May 1692 a new governor for the colony of Massachusetts arrived from England. William Phips brought with him an up-to-date charter to replace the one that had expired three years before. Without the new charter, any courts set up to deal with the more than 100 accused witches in Massachusetts jails would not have had any real authority.

Oyer and Terminer

Phips quickly authorized a special emergency legal process called a Court of Oyer and Terminer (which in Latin means "to hear and to decide"). He appointed nine judges to hear the cases of the accused Salem witches. In addition to John Hathorne and Jonathan Corwin, who had served as magistrates throughout the hearings, Phips selected Samuel Sewall, Bartholomew Gedney, John Richards, Nathaniel Saltonstall, Peter Sergeant, and Wait Still Winthrop. He chose his lieutenant governor, William Stoughton, to be chief justice. Phips was astonished by the number of accused witches and by the nature of their supposed evil deeds. He wrote later that the province seemed to be "miserably harassed with a most horrible witchcraft or possession of devils. . . . Scores of poor people were taken with preternatural torments, some scalded with brimstone, some had stuck pins in their flesh, others hurried into the fire and water, and some [were] dragged out of their houses and carried over the tops of trees and hills for many miles together."[55]

Though aware of the overflowing jails, Phips had a more practical reason for wanting to speed up the trial process. Prisoners—no matter what crimes they were accused of—were expected to pay the costs of their lodging, which included food, firewood, and even the chains used to secure their arms to the walls. If the trials did not begin soon, many of the prisoners would find the financial burden so extraordinarily high that the jailers would never be able to collect so large a sum of money.

Establishing Rules

Just before the trials began, Richards wrote a letter to Cotton Mather about what sorts of evidence Mather believed should be admissible in court. For instance, the hearings had been largely based on the testimony of the afflicted girls, whose stories of specters and evil acts could not be corroborated because few of these acts had been seen by anyone else. Richards wondered if it was fair to allow such testimony to be allowed as evidence against an accused person.

Mather wrote back that though he believed spectral evidence could be helpful, he was uncomfortable with relying too much upon it in court:

> I must most humbly beg you that . . . you do not lay more stress upon pure Spectre testimony than it will bear. . . . It is very certain that the devils have sometimes represented the shapes of persons not only innocent but also very virtuous. . . . Moreover, I do suspect that the persons, who have too much indulged themselves in malignant, envious, malicious ebullitions [outbursts] of their souls, may unhappily expose themselves to the judgment of being represented by devils, of whom they never had any vision, and with whom they have had much less written a covenant.[56]

Mather also urged the court to think seriously about having a punishment for convicted witches that was less severe than death. However, neither of his suggestions was adopted, as the new court's first case demonstrated.

The Case of Bridget Bishop

Though the Court of Oyer and Terminer was official, it ended up being as chaotic as the hearings had been. Spectators were allowed to shout out comments about the accused. Contrary to Mather's advice, spectral evidence was given great importance in the trials, as it had been at the hearings. Stoughton, acting as chief justice of the court, disagreed with Mather and insisted that if the devil appeared in the shape of someone, there was no possibility that that person could be innocent. And just as in the earlier hearings, the afflicted girls were present—convulsing, screaming, and writhing on the floor when any of the accused testified.

The court began with the case of Bridget Bishop. Bishop was a gregarious woman who owned a tavern and allowed young people to play loud games of shuffleboard long into the late hours. She also liked bright colors, occasionally wearing a red bodice looped with other bright colors—very flashy for a time when women were expected to wear drab colors and plain styles. Because she was so different from most Puritan women, some in town had previously suspected her of being a witch.

Some of those who testified against her at trial claimed she could assume the shape of animals, while others said they had seen her with a cat thought to be her familiar. What little sympathy she evoked among the townspeople was essentially wiped out by an unexplainable occurrence that happened on the way to the town meetinghouse for the trial. Just as Bishop glanced at the meetinghouse, the guards accompanying her heard a loud clatter, and a heavy beam fell down. Investigators who looked into the odd event said they found "a board which was strongly fastened with several nails transported into another quarter of the house."[57]

With such evidence, it did not take long for the jury of 12 men to find Bishop guilty. She was sentenced to be executed and was hanged in

Townspeople jeer as Bridget Bishop—standing in a wooden cart with her hands bound—is readied for hanging. Bishop's gregarious personality, late-night hours, and fondness for wearing bright colors aroused suspicion among her Puritan neighbors.

Salem Town on June 10, 1692. Historians agree that some of the judges attended this first execution. One of the judges, Saltonstall, was so upset by the hanging that he immediately resigned his post. Saltonstall was later accused of witchcraft, though he was not convicted.

The Tragedy of Rebecca Nurse

Bishop's trial was followed on June 30 with the trials of five more women, including Sarah Good and Rebecca Nurse. All five were convicted and sentenced to hang. Many historians point to Nurse's conviction as the prime example of the tragic consequences of the witchcraft panic.

Nurse, the frail, elderly woman who had been targeted by the afflicted girls, was championed by dozens of citizens of Salem Village. Before the trial, 39 people signed a petition vouching for Nurse, saying that she had led "her life and conversation . . . according to her profession [of faith]," and that they had never had "any cause or grounds to suspect her of anything as she is now accused."[58]

For a while it looked as though Nurse would be acquitted of the charges against her. The jury seemed to feel that she had been unreasonably targeted and that her accusers had been mistaken. They found her not guilty of the charges. However, Stoughton, the chief justice, was unconvinced of her innocence. He asked the jury to reconsider its verdict.

When reinterviewed, Nurse stared straight ahead when a member of the jury asked her a question. Stoughton and others believed she was avoiding answering the question, but many historians point out that because she was partially deaf, she likely did not even hear the question. Her silence was taken as a refusal to answer, and combined with the renewed convulsing and shrieking of the afflicted girls, Nurse was convicted and sentenced to be hanged.

The Horror of Executions

The hangings of those found guilty of witchcraft in Salem were carried out in the same way as witch hangings in Europe. Though no one knows positively where the hanging site was in Salem, many historians believe it was on what has come to be known through the years as Gallows Hill, a large slope just inland from Salem Town.

Personal accounts from that time indicate that the condemned were transported to the site in wooden carts, their feet and hands securely chained. Some of the prisoners were so frightened or ill that they could not stand, but rather slumped to the floor of the cart. Along the route, the afflicted girls mocked them, and other spectators walked or ran alongside the carts, shouting insults at the victims.

When the cart reached its destination—a sturdy tree, with one or more nooses hanging from its branches—the executioner carried or otherwise accompanied each victim up a ladder and looped the noose around the victim's neck. A cloth hood was put over the victim's head to protect the crowd from the gruesome sight of what was often a slow, tortuous death. One by one, the executioner pushed each convicted witch from the ladder. Many hanging victims dangled in agony for as long as 10 minutes before they finally died. Once pronounced dead, the victims were cut down and their bodies were tossed into a shallow grave. They were treated with as little civility in death as they had been in the last days of life.

The Panic Spreads

As the trials and executions continued, the witchcraft fever seemed to increase—and spread. People in nearby towns and villages were being accused of being witches, too. In nearby Andover, Massachusetts, a woman named Elizabeth Ballard had been bedridden with an unknown ailment. Doctors seemed unable to find a cause, and someone suggested that, like some in Salem Village, she may have been bewitched.

To learn whether witchcraft was the cause, her husband Joseph asked two of the afflicted girls, Ann Putnam and Mary Walcott, to come to Andover in mid-July 1692 to find out who was at fault for his wife's condition. The girls named several people in Andover, and within several days more than 40 others were accused of having made a pact with the devil, causing Ballard to fall ill.

As the weeks went by, the number of people accused of witchcraft grew even more quickly than before. Many believed that by accusing someone else of being a witch, they themselves were less likely to be targeted.

Options

Those who were accused of witchcraft had a choice: They could maintain their innocence and, if found guilty (as almost all were), be hanged. Or they could confess and spend the rest of their lives in jail (because

A Rare Escape

Though she had no idea why, Elizabeth Cary was accused of witchcraft by the two afflicted girls and was sent to prison to await her sentence. Her husband Nathaniel was astonished at the inhumane treatment she received. "Having been there one night, next morning the jailer put irons on her legs, having received such a command," he wrote later. "The weight of them was about eight pounds. These irons and her other afflictions soon brought her into convulsive fits, so I thought she would have died that night. I sent to entreat that their irons might be taken off, but all entreaties were in vain . . . so in this condition she must continue."

Though Nathaniel Cary considered himself a law-abiding citizen, he realized that his wife would either die in prison or be hanged. He begged that she be tried in another county by other judges but was told that was impossible. Finally, as a last resort, he helped her escape in early July—most likely by bribing the jailers. The couple fled to Rhode Island but eventually went back to Massachusetts when the Salem trials ended.

Quoted in Frances Hill, *A Delusion of Satan: The Full Story of the Salem Witch Trials.* Cambridge, MA: Da Capo, 1995, p. 142.

judges of the time were uneasy about sentencing someone to death who admitted their crimes). This is why many of the accused admitted to witchcraft; their families and friends begged them to confess so that they would not be executed. These prisoners often created intricate stories that named others as taking part in witchcraft, too. And of course, every newly named person had to make the same decision: to confess and live for an indeterminate time in the gruesome conditions of seventeenth-century jails or tell the truth and die.

With each new confession the witchcraft panic gained momentum. Judges, magistrates, and the general public viewed the growing number of confessions as proof that they had been correct in aggressively prosecuting suspected witches. The confessions also reinforced belief in the ability of the afflicted girls to root out witchcraft. Jailers tortured prisoners who did not want to confess to the lies told about them. Women were humiliated by being forced to disrobe so that a magistrate or jailer could search for a "witch's teat"—any growth such as a mole or wart that a witch could use to feed a familiar.

Most of the tortures were meant to get the accused to confess or accuse someone else. One of the methods sometimes used was called "tying neck and heels." A prisoner's heels and neck were tightly tied to each other, with knees bent and heels behind the body to form a backward bow, or as Frances Hill notes, their bodies "were forced into hoops, necks roped to feet."[59] Accused witches were tied in that manner and left for hours at a time. One man wrote about his son, who was tortured that way: "My son William . . . when he was examined, because he would not confess that he was guilty when he was innocent, they tied him neck and heels till the blood gushed out of his nose, and would have kept him so 24 hours, if one more merciful than the rest had not taken pity on him, and caused him to be unbound."[60]

A Humble Plea

Other instances of human kindness—or perhaps pity—surfaced as the trials wore on. Such was the case with 58-year-old Mary Easty (sometimes spelled Esty), a younger sister of Nurse, who was firm in her denial of being a witch. During her examination, she had impressed the magistrates—even the irascible Hathorne—as a kind, thoughtful woman who was genuinely puzzled by the charges against her. And though she was sent to jail to await trial (the afflicted girls were certain she was a witch), even the jailers took up her cause, suggesting to the magistrates that they change their verdict.

Though she was eventually condemned to hang on September 22, Easty asked to be allowed to speak before she was executed. Poised and calm, she read an appeal—not for herself but for future prisoners who would stand trial:

> I petition to your honours, not for my own life, for I know I must die, and my appointed time is set, but the Lord he knows it is, if it be possible, that no more innocent blood be shed, which undoubtedly cannot be avoided in the way and course you go in. . . . I would humbly beg of you that your Honours would be pleased to examine some of the confessing witches, I being confident there are several of them have belied themselves and others, as will appear, if not in this world, I am sure in the world to come, whither I am going; and I question not, but yourselves will see an alteration in these things. They say myself and others have made a League with the devil, we cannot confess. I know and the Lord he knows (as will shortly appear) they belie me. . . . I know not the least thing of witchcraft; therefore I cannot, I durst not belye my soul.[61]

"More Weight"

One prisoner who refused to confess also refused even to participate in his own trial. He was 80-year-old Giles Corey, the husband of convicted witch Martha Corey. He had been looked at with suspicion when she was accused, but he had testified against her, claiming that when his wife was near him he was unable to pray. He was eventually arrested and jailed.

Unlike the others, Corey did not appear before the Court of Oyer and Terminer after his initial hearing, because he refused to speak when asked whether he pleaded guilty or innocent. He did not trust the judges to be fair or just. Historians say he might have had another reason for wanting to avoid a trial. Corey owned a valuable piece of land in Salem Village. Laws in those days made it illegal for one convicted of a crime to will his property to his children when he died. Instead, the court could confiscate the convicted criminal's belongings—including land.

Corey was aware that a guilty verdict against him was likely if he went to trial, and he had no intention of letting that happen.

He took advantage of a law that said a suspect who did not enter a plea—either guilty or innocent—could not be tried in court. No matter how many times they asked him, no matter how hard they tried to persuade him, the judges could not get Corey to give them any plea at all. Because they could not try Corey, court officials imposed a sentence of *peine forte et dure*—torture to force a prisoner to change his mind. To carry out the sentence, says Suffolk University history professor Robert J. Allison, court officials forced Corey to lie on a stone slab with two boards on his chest and then gradually "pressed" him to death: "Stones are placed on the boards—making a heavier and heavier weight to squeeze him to death, to squeeze a confession out of him. The court surrounds [Corey] as he is lying there. This goes on for about two days as more and more weight is put on Giles Corey's chest. Every time they ask: 'Are you ready to confess?' he says: 'More weight' until he is crushed to death."[62]

A Turning Point

The torturous death of Corey shocked many Massachusetts citizens, and like the appeal made on behalf of Easty, it marked another turning point in attitudes toward the witchcraft trials. By the end of September 1692—seven months after the first women in Salem Village were accused—many people had begun to think again about the legitimacy of the witch trials.

They thought about the numbers of seemingly good, religious people who had been accused, convicted, and executed. It seemed to make little sense that so many witches could have been living among them for so long. As John Hale, a pastor from nearby Beverly, noted, "It cannot be imagined that in a place of so much knowledge, so many in so small compass of land should abominably leap into the Devil's lap at once."[63]

After the September 22 executions, the Court of Oyer and Terminer was adjourned, although the judges intended that it would reconvene in a month or two. The jails were still full to bursting with people

An accused witch seated on a ducking stool is repeatedly dunked in water. Accused witches were often tortured to obtain confessions or elicit the names of others who might be influenced by the devil.

accused of witchcraft, but public opinion was undergoing a dramatic change.

Winding Down the Witch Trials

The afflicted girls continued to convulse and writhe when certain people came into view, but their targets had become more and more unbelievable. For example, they called out Hale and Lady Phips (the wife of Governor William Phips) as witches in late September and

A Prayer Said Well

When former minister George Burroughs was about to be hanged on August 19, 1692, he spoke eloquently to the gathered crowd and then recited the Lord's Prayer without a single mistake—something that witches were said to be incapable of doing. After the hanging, the influential minister Cotton Mather explained the seeming inconsistency as a trick of the devil rather than a sign of Burroughs's innocence. The scene is described in Frances Hill's *The Salem Witch Trials Reader.*

Mr. Burroughs was carried in a cart with the others through the streets of Salem to execution; when he was upon the ladder, he made a speech for the clearing of his innocency, with such solemn and serious expressions, as were to the admiration of all present; his prayer (which he concluded by repeating the Lord's prayer) was so well worded, and uttered with such composedness, and such (at least seeming) fervency of spirit, as was very affecting, and drew tears from many. . . . As soon as he was turned off [killed], Mr. Cotton Mather, being mounted upon a horse, addressed himself to the people, partly to declare that [Burroughs] was no ordained minister, and partly to possess the people of his guilt; saying, that the devil has often been transformed into an angel of the light.

Frances Hill, *The Salem Witch Trials Reader.* Cambridge, MA: Da Capo, 2001, p. 76.

early October 1692. By this time, however, most people had lost their appetite for witch-hunting and the girls were largely ignored.

On October 12, Phips announced that he was halting what he referred to as "the black cloud that threatened this province with destruction" and admitted that "this delusion of the devil did spread and its dismal effects touched the lives and estates of many of their Majesty's subjects . . . and indeed unhappily clogged and interrupted their Majesty's affairs," which was, Phips said, "a great vexation to me."[64] Phips ordered those prisoners still languishing in prisons to be dismissed as soon as their jail fees were paid. He also granted a reprieve to those who had been found guilty and were awaiting execution.

The finger-pointing and the accusations of witchcraft had ceased with the official ending of the Court of Oyer and Terminer and the pardon of those still in prison, but the nightmare of the Salem witch trials was not really over. The bitter feelings, grief, and distrust people felt during those months of examinations and trials would continue to surface for years to come.

Chapter 5

What Is the Legacy of the Salem Witch Trials?

When the last executions of the Salem witch trials were carried out on September 22, 1692, the official count stood at 19 people hanged and one pressed to death. Sarah Good, the first to be accused, delivered a baby that died in jail. Four others awaiting execution died in jail, too, including Sarah Osborne, who was already in poor health when she was tried.

But the damage cannot be measured only in the death count. The victims left families behind, most of them angry and confused by the accusations that ensnared their loved ones. Dorcas Good, the four-year-old who was jailed with her mother, was a good example of how damaging accusations were to the children of accused witches. Though Dorcas was eventually released, she was never the same. According to her father, William Good, the little girl suffered from mental illness for the rest of her life. Dorcas, her father wrote, "was in prison seven or eight months and being chained in the dungeon was so hardly used and terrified that she hath ever since been very changeable, having little or no reason to govern herself."[65]

Lingering Bitterness
Besides the tragic deaths and sorrow of the victims and their families, there was damage to the fabric of the community, too, for many

people whose families were torn apart were resentful. Many who had fled Salem returned later to find their farms and homes ransacked and their possessions either repossessed or pilfered by neighbors. After the trials ended, they would spend years trying to reclaim what they had lost.

In their anger and resentment, the victims blamed the judges, the magistrates, and most of all, the villagers who pointed the fingers of guilt at their loved ones. And for almost all of the people of Salem, there would be the lingering questions of why this happened, how things could have spiraled so terribly out of control, and how a God-fearing Puritan community could have turned on its own with such a vengeance.

In the centuries since the Salem witch trials, historians have attempted to answer those same questions, trying to explain how the accusations of the three girls could have whipped up a frenzy that resulted in so many deaths and imprisonments. Looking back from a vantage point more than 300 years afterward, it seems almost preposterous that so many of the citizens of Salem Village could have believed in the validity of the convulsions and visions of these girls.

Salem witch trial expert Diane E. Foulds suggests that the trials might have been a desperate attempt by Salem villagers to control the harsh and unforgiving nature of their daily existence. The lives of the Puritans in the late seventeenth century were filled with fear and anxiety over things that were far beyond their control—terrible diseases, Indian attacks, and bad weather destroying their crops—coupled with the constraints of a rigid religion. Foulds says, "Today we can only wonder how such seasoned judges could have believed the frenzied slurs of the 'afflicted' children. Perhaps . . . they willfully ignored the obvious truth because it seemed like one disturbance that they could control."[66]

Hysteria as an Explanation

Some historians speculate that the afflicted girls were experiencing clinical hysteria, perhaps brought on by the fears and rigidity of their

A guilty verdict is pronounced in the trial of an accused witch in Salem. When the trials finally ended, families torn apart by the events of 1692 blamed the judges, the magistrates, and, most of all, the townspeople for their unconscionable acts.

society. It is possible, experts say, that the convulsions, babbling, seizures, and other behaviors resulted from some type of hysteria. In his 1882 book, *The Psychology of the Salem Witchcraft Excitement of 1692*, George Beard theorized that the afflicted girls were so excited and overstimulated by the Puritans' fixation on the devil that they became "partly insane and partly entranced."[67]

Other historians disagree, insisting that the girls' behavior was not the result of mental illness, but rather a form of playacting. They suggest that after dabbling in the games of witchcraft with Tituba, the games continued and then escalated beyond anything they had imagined. By the time trials were being held and people whom they had accused were being imprisoned, the game had gone too far for the girls to admit what they had done. And the townspeople—incited by Samuel Parris and other town leaders—seemed willing to go along with it.

John Hale, who had supported the trials at first, later wrote of "the sad consequences of mistakes" and the "grief of heart . . . to have been encouraging of the sufferings of the innocent."[68] Hale was unable to explain how it all came about, other than pointing to the mob mentality and chaos of the times. "But such was the darkness of that day," he wrote, "the tortures and lamentations of the afflicted, and the power of former precedents, that we walked in the clouds, and could not see our way."[69]

Apologies

The terrible events that took place in Salem in 1692 began with a few girls but grew to far larger proportions, thanks to the people of Salem. From Parris, whose sermons whipped up action against the accused witches, to the judges who allowed spectral evidence in court, to the townspeople who shouted for convictions, and to the jailers who abused their prisoners—many individuals played a role in these extraordinary events.

Even so, apologies were few, and it was years before they were offered. Notes Frances Hill, "Remorse was thin on the ground altogether in the aftermath. . . . At no point was there clear, universal recognition that a huge wrong had been done and that the instigators of the witchcraft prosecutions were the wrongdoers."[70] One group that did express remorse was that of the 12 men who had sat on several juries for the trials. On January 14, 1697, a day that had been set aside as a day of fasting to atone for sins and mistakes made—including the witch trials—the jurors signed a paper expressing their apology, stating, "We confess that we ourselves were not capable to understand, nor able to withstand the mysterious delusions of the powers of darkness and prince of the air. . . . We do heartily ask forgiveness of you all, whom we have justly offended, and do declare according to our present minds, we would none of us do such things again on such grounds for the whole world."[71]

Judge Samuel Sewall, too, felt afterward that he had made a terrible mistake. On that same day, he stood in his church, head bowed, while his minister read aloud the letter of apology the judge had written. In the letter, Sewall admitted his mistakes and begged forgiveness. He desired, he wrote, "to take the blame and shame" of "the opening of the late Comission of Oyer and Terminer at Salem," and asked that God "not visit the sin of him, or any other upon himself or any of his, nor upon the land."[72] Sewall felt so much remorse that once a year for the rest of his life he observed his own day of fasting in penance for the suffering he had caused.

The End of Spectral Evidence

It is difficult to point to any positive outcomes of the Salem witch trials, but there is at least one. From this point forward, no courts in colonial America allowed the use of spectral evidence. No longer

A War-Time Witch Hunt

In 1941, soon after the Japanese attack on Pearl Harbor, President Franklin D. Roosevelt signed Executive Order 1066. The order in effect deprived more than 110,000 people of Japanese descent of the protections guaranteed them under the US Constitution. The detainees—including many children—were either US citizens or legal permanent residents. Despite their legal status, they were evacuated from their homes by members of the US military and incarcerated for four years in relocation camps. The point of this relocation was to prevent espionage and sabotage by Japanese who might feel allegiance to their homeland during the war.

Surrounded by barbed wire and guarded by armed soldiers, the camps were located in remote areas of Arizona, California, Idaho, Wyoming, Colorado, and Utah. They were very primitive, without running water or adequate sanitation. It was not uncommon for 25 detainees to be living in a space designed for four people.

Fifty years later, in 1988, Congress passed the Civil Liberties Act of 1988, apologizing for the relocation. President Bill Clinton sent a letter of apology to each of the living survivors, with a check for $20,000. In part, the President wrote, "the nation's actions were rooted deeply in racial prejudice, wartime hysteria, and a lack of political leadership."

Quoted in PBS.org, "Children of the Camps." www.pbs.org.

could someone claim to have seen something that was invisible to others and present it as evidence in a court proceeding. The afflicted girls had done this time after time, both in their recollections of the accused and in their insistence during the trials that they could see specters in the courtroom.

Because such dubious evidence was responsible for the conviction of a large number of the accused, many believed it should be banned from courtrooms. They heartily agreed with Increase Mather, who wrote a paper in 1693 titled *Cases of Conscience Concerning Evil Spirits* that criticized the practice of using spectral evidence in court. If the only way to convict someone of witchcraft was through spectral evidence, Mather stated, it was better to allow that person to go free. "It were better that ten suspected witches should escape," he wrote, "than one innocent person should be condemned."[73]

Witch Fears Winding Down

The most fitting legacy of the Salem witch trials might have been an end to witch hunts, where fear and mistrust lead to accusations, ruined reputations, and death. Though there were no further executions of people accused of being witches, Salem was not the last witch hunt in the American colonies.

As the Salem trials were winding down late in 1692, two Connecticut women, Mercy Disborough and Elizabeth Clawson, were tried for bewitching a 17-year-old servant named Katherine Branch. According to historian Brian Pavlac, the teen suffered "fits of pain and believed that cats spoke to her, [and] hurt her."[74] The court found there was not enough evidence to convict the women.

Several other cases of alleged witchcraft never made it to court. In 1746 the Reverend Peter Clark of Salem Village charged that some members of his congregation had consulted with women who claimed to be fortune-tellers. Clark fervently advised the people of his parish about what he called "the infamous and ungodly practice of witches and fortune-tellers or any that are reputed such," and he urged those who had done so "to repent and return to God, earnestly seeking forgivenenss."[75]

By the nineteenth century witchcraft allegations had lessened dramatically. Strides in science and medicine were providing explanations for diseases and crop failures, which meant that fewer people blamed witches or the devil for such hardships. Little by little, rampant fear of witchcraft was becoming a thing of the past.

The Modern Witch Hunt

Possibly the most important legacy of the Salem witch trials is a lesson in the ways in which group dynamics can contribute to the persecution of individuals. The term *witch hunt* has come to be used metaphorically to describe a situation in which a community or agency rushes to judgment, persecuting people based on rumor, innuendo, or what is sometimes called "the court of public opinion" rather than on facts. Historians say the Salem witch trials have served as a cautionary tale for later generations—although the lessons of the events in Salem in 1692 have not always been heeded.

Modern witch hunts have occurred during times of fear and uncertainty. The most famous witch hunt in modern American history occurred in the late 1940s and early 1950s. During that period thousands of people were accused of being Communists or Communist sympathizers, though neither one of those was actually a crime. Even so, some of those accused lost their jobs and reputations, and many went to jail after being interrogated. People who were accused were presumed guilty and were forced to prove they were innocent—the reverse of what the American form of justice promises.

Communism was the economic system of the Soviet Union, the former federation of republics throughout Eastern Europe and central and northern Asia. Though the Soviets fought on the same side as the United States during World War II, after the war the two countries became sworn enemies. The Soviet Union, which was ruled by an authoritarian government, vowed to spread communism throughout the world and to defeat the United States by any means possible. The United States strongly opposed the Communist system and the lack of personal freedoms in the Soviet Union and sought to block communism's spread. The two nations did not engage in direct military conflict. Rather, they waged what was called the Cold War—exchanging angry words, spying on one another, cultivating allies among other countries, and building up their arsenals of traditional and nuclear weapons.

In those post–World War II years, Americans feared that Soviet Communists were plotting their demise. Being labeled a Communist— or even a Communist sympathizer—in the United States was virtually the same as being called a traitor. Those years, recalls retired Minnesota health-care worker Doris Eberhardt, were very frightening, as Americans worried about Communists in their midst. "I was a young girl back then growing up with my brothers and sister on a farm down in southern Minnesota," she says.

> I was never as afraid of anything as I was of Communists. We would hear on the radio about [the Soviets] storming into those places in Eastern Europe, and taking over. They'd turn everyone into communists. I certainly remember being frightened at all the talk. Terrified, I think is more like it. We'd hear our parents talking about it, and I got the impression they were very nervous. As a girl, I had nightmares about them coming across the ocean with their tanks and guns to take over our farm and turning us all into Communists, too. . . . It's hard today to imagine people so frightened about something like that, but we really were.[76]

Suspicions and Fears

The fear of communism and the hostility between the United States and the Soviet Union were so intense that it seemed crucial for American leaders to make certain that no Communists or Communist sympathizers worked for the US government. The House of Representatives established the House Committee on Un-American Activities (known as HCUA) to investigate subversive activities that might threaten the security of the United States. In 1947 President Harry Truman launched a massive security program, investigating millions of federal employees. None were found to be Soviet spies, but that did not calm the nation's fears about Communists.

The hunt for Communists did not end with federal workers. In that climate of fear, anyone could be suspected of being a Communist or a Communist sympathizer. Labor union leaders who advocated for expanded rights for American workers were suspect, as were African

A Memorial in Salem

In 1992, the three hundredth anniversary of the Salem witch trials, a memorial park in Salem, Massachusetts, was dedicated to commemorate the victims of the witch hunt—20 people who had been put to death because of fear, superstition, and a failed court system. With a grant from the National Endowment for the Arts, the park was created as a reminder of the consequences of the trials. There are 20 stone benches, each inscribed with the name of one of the victims, as well as the date and means of his or her execution. The park also features stones inscribed with the words of each of the victims as they protested their innocence moments before their death.

The park was dedicated on August 5, 1992, by Holocaust survivor and Nobel Prize–winning author Elie Wiesel. Also in attendance was Arthur Miller, one of the writers unjustly accused of being a Communist sympathizer during the McCarthy era. Miller wrote *The Crucible*, comparing McCarthyism to the Salem witch trials. As of 2011 the park in Salem had received more than 7 million visitors.

Americans, Jews, and any immigrants from Eastern European countries controlled by the Soviet Union. Those who advocated peace talks with the Soviets were considered "soft" on communism—and therefore sympathizers—even if they were not Communists themselves.

Epitome of a Modern Witch-Hunter

Into this climate of almost paralyzing fear stepped Joseph McCarthy, a little-known Republican senator from Wisconsin. McCarthy, more than anyone since the Salem trials, has come to symbolize the modern-day witch hunter. As a result of McCarthy's efforts, between 1950 and 1954 hundreds of Americans were accused of being Communist spies or sympathizers.

In 1950 some friends suggested that McCarthy grab the spotlight by going after Communists. He had done very little during his first term in office, and this sounded like a good way to get some attention while campaigning for a second term. According to McCarthy biographer Richard H. Rovere, McCarthy responded by saying, "That's it. The government is full of communists. We can hammer away at them."[77]

He began his campaign against people alleged to be Communists in a speech to a women's group in West Virginia in February 1950. During the speech, McCarthy held up a sheet of paper and announced to a dumbstruck audience, "I have here in my hand a list of 205 that were known to the Secretary of State as being members of the Communist Party and who, nevertheless, are still working and shaping policy of the State Department."[78]

The paper contained no such names; what McCarthy held up was actually his laundry list. But it was such a bold announcement that it became the top story in the next morning's newspapers and ignited fears about Communists in the United States. McCarthy gave numerous speeches about the dangers the American people faced from Communists in their midst. He continued his allegations, claiming he knew that certain people in the government were Soviet spies, Communists, or Communist sympathizers.

Republicans Against Democrats

As with the events in Salem in 1692, the climate of fear in the United States in the early 1950s made his preposterous statements believable to many Americans. Under the leadership of McCarthy, the Senate held hearings to investigate his claims. Though he had no evidence to support any of his accusations, McCarthy and his Republican political colleagues reaped the benefits, for most of those they targeted were Democrats. Those whom McCarthy accused were investigated and embarrassed publicly. Most lost their jobs, their homes, and their reputations. Those who questioned his tactics or objected to his accusations were likely to find themselves charged with being soft on communism—a charge that clearly implied traitorous views.

Even members of the press were sometimes willing to accept McCarthy's statements without question. For example, instead of asking for evidence to support McCarthy's list of 205 alleged Communists in the State Department, North Carolina's *Charlotte Observer* insisted that the senator would never have accused people unless he had proof, saying, "It is unbelievable that a U.S. Senator would publicly and repeatedly make such charges if he did not have any evidence to support them."[79] Even though McCarthy never provided a shred of proof

At a 1951 hearing, Senator Joseph McCarthy (seated at left) accuses a nominee for a United Nations post of being a Communist sympathizer. McCarthy spent four years trying to root out Communists in government and the arts—a campaign that has been likened to a modern-day witch hunt.

against any of the people he accused, he remained a popular figure at a time when fear of communism was high.

Only after McCarthy began questioning the integrity and loyalty of members of the military did his power dissolve. In 1954 the Senate hearings led by McCarthy were televised, and for the first time millions of Americans got to see him in action. The public was shocked as they watched him bully and humiliate members of the military and accuse them of engaging in subversive activities—while presenting no evidence of their guilt. McCarthy's approval rating plummeted, and in December 1954 the Senate voted 67 to 22 to censure him. His name lives on in the infamous term *McCarthyism*, which is the accusation of treason or disloyalty without evidence.

A Twenty-First-Century Witch Hunt?

Witch hunts in the United States did not stop with McCarthyism. Many believe that after the terrorist attacks on the United States on September 11, 2001, another witch hunt began. Not surprisingly, fear and panic were widespread. Never had there been an attack on the United States of that magnitude, and the nation was horrified.

The attacks had come without warning, and though nearly 3,000 people were killed that day, it seemed that the entire country had been victimized. When investigators learned that the hijackers were part of the radical Islamic terrorist group al Qaeda, the horror and fury felt by Americans erupted into several episodes of violence aimed at individuals of the Muslim faith or those mistaken for Muslims. Just days after the 9/11 attacks, a Hindu service station owner in New York was shot by a man who told police that he mistook the victim for a Muslim. A Virginia woman wearing a traditional Muslim head scarf was severely injured by a driver who admitted that he plowed into her on purpose. Throughout the United States police reported attacks and threats—both verbal and physical—against people who looked like they might be Muslim or from the Arab-speaking world from which the terrorists had come.

The USA PATRIOT Act and Guantánamo Bay

Within weeks of the 9/11 attacks, Congress passed a law called the USA PATRIOT Act, which President George W. Bush signed into law on October 26, 2001. The new law, supported by both Democrats and Republicans, granted the government sweeping new powers. Under this law the government could conduct electronic surveillance on citizens and hold suspects in secret for weeks or months without charging them—both contrary to rights guaranteed under the US Constitution.

More than 700 people suspected of being part of or helping the group that carried out the 9/11 attacks were rounded up in various countries and taken to the US military prison in Cuba, at Guantánamo Bay Naval Base. Their names were not released, so no one—including their families—knew where they were. Some were subjected to torture in order to get confessions from them.

Reaction to the PATRIOT Act was mixed. Some Americans believed that the nature of the threat against the United States, as illustrated by the 9/11 attacks, justified these types of measures. In a hearing before the House Judiciary Committee on September 24, 2001, Attorney General John Ashcroft warned that the legislation had to be passed in order to prevent further attacks.

The American people do not have the luxury of unlimited time in erecting the necessary defenses to future terrorist acts. The danger that darkened the United States of America and the civilized world on September 11 did not pass with the atrocities committed that day. They require that we provide law enforcement with the tools necessary to identify, dismantle, disrupt, and punish terrorist organizations before they strike again.[80]

Others, however, felt strongly that the powers granted the government under the PATRIOT Act violated rights guaranteed under the US Constitution. During the 2001 congressional debate on the bill,

Wisconsin senator Russ Feingold cautioned against forgetting the lessons of the past:

> There have been periods in our nation's history when civil liberties have taken a back seat to what appeared at the time to be legitimate exigencies [urgent needs] of war. Our national consciousness still bears the stain and the scars of those events . . . [including] the internment of Japanese-Americans, German-Americans, and Italian-Americans during World War II, the blacklisting of supposed communist sympathizers during the McCarthy era, and the surveillance and harassment of antiwar protesters, including Dr. Martin Luther King, Jr., during the Vietnam War. We must not allow these pieces of our past to become prologue.[81]

The Lesson of Salem

Witch hunts flourish in an environment of fear and panic and are usually led by people who claim to be trying to protect their community. However, when such actions occur—as in seventeenth-century Salem, in 1950s America, or after 9/11, says Robert Rapley, they can take on a life of their own, growing "out of control like forest fires. The innocent get swept up with the guilty. Torture becomes accepted as a tool of protection for society and of attack against the 'evil ones.'"[82] And with the advantage of hindsight, it is easy to see that the price society pays for this protection is always far too high.

Source Notes

Introduction: The Defining Characteristics of the Salem Witch Trials

1. Quoted in Elizabeth Reis, *Damned Women: Sinners and Witches in Puritan New England*. Ithaca, NY: Cornell University Press, 1997, p. 19.
2. Richard Weisman, *Witchcraft, Magic, and Religion in 17th Century Massachusetts*. Amherst: University of Massachusetts Press, 1984, p. 121.
3. *Malleus Maleficarum Part I,* Internet Sacred Text Archive. www.sacred-texts.com.
4. Robin Briggs, *Witches and Neighbours*. Malden, MA: Blackwell, 2002, p. 6.

Chapter One: What Conditions Led to the Salem Witch Trials?

5. John Winthrop, "A Model of Christian Charity," 1630, Religious Freedom Page. http://religiousfreedom.lib.virginia.edu.
6. Quoted in History Channel, *Salem Witch Trials*. New York: A&E Home Video, 2005, DVD.
7. Quoted in History Channel, *Salem Witch Trials*.
8. Quoted in Frances Hill, *A Delusion of Satan: The Full Story of the Salem Witch Trials*. New York: Da Capo, 1995, p. 8.
9. Hill, *A Delusion of Satan*, p. 5.
10. Quoted in Michael G. Hall, *The Last American Puritan: The Life of Increase Mather*. Middletown, CT: Wesleyan University Press, 1988, p. 5.
11. Quoted in V.F. Calverton, *The Awakening of America*. New York: John Day, 1939, p. 122.
12. Hill, *A Delusion of Satan*, p. 10.

13. Quoted in Joel Parker, *The First Charter and the Early Religious Legislation of Massachusetts.* Boston: John Wilson and Son, 1869, pp. 74–75.

14. Quoted in Mayflower and Early Families, "The Quakers: 'Hostile Bonnets and Gowns.'" www.mayflowerfamilies.com.

15. Horatio Rogers, *Mary Dyer of Rhode Island, the Quaker Martyr That Was Hanged on Boston Common, June 1, 1660.* Providence, RI: Preston and Rounds, 1896, p. 4.

16. Quoted in Peter Oliver, *The Puritan Commonwealth: An Historical Review of the Puritan Government in Massachusetts in Its Civil and Ecclesiastical Relations.* Boston: Little, Brown, 1856, p. 40.

17. Robert Rapley, *Witch Hunts: From Salem to Guantanamo Bay.* Montreal: McGill-Queen's University Press, 2007, pp. 63–64.

Chapter Two: Murmurs and Accusations

18. Quoted in Frances Hill, *The Salem Witch Trials Reader.* Cambridge, MA: Da Capo, 2001, p. 19.

19. Quoted in Goody Glover's, "Goodwife 'Goody' Ann Glover." www.goodyglovers.com.

20. William J. Birnes and Joel Martin, *The Haunting of America: From the Salem Witch Trials to Harry Houdini.* New York: Doherty, 2009, p. 69.

21. Quoted in Hill, *A Delusion of Satan*, p. 14.

22. Quoted in David Goss, *The Salem Witch Trials: A Reference Guide.* Westport, CT: Greenwood, 2008, p. 17.

23. Quoted in Hill, *The Salem Witch Trials Reader*, p. 59.

24. Quoted in Richard Ling, "Cyber-McCarthyism: Witch Hunts in the Living Room," *Electronic Journal of Sociology*, 1996. www.sociology.org.

25. Exodus 22:18 (King James Version.)

26. 1 Peter 5:8 (King James Version).

27. Quoted in Larry Gragg, *The Salem Witch Crisis.* New York: Praeger, 1992, p. 46.

28. Hill, *A Delusion of Satan*, p. 24,

29. Quoted in Hill, *A Delusion of Satan*, p. 25.

30. Quoted in Hill, *A Delusion of Satan*, p. 25.

31. Quoted in George Lincoln Burr, ed., *Narratives of the Witchcraft Cases, 1648–1706*. New York: Barnes, 1914, p. 413.

32. Kai T. Erikson, *Wayward Puritans: A Study in the Sociology of Deviance*. New York: Wiley, 1966, pp. 143–44.

Chapter Three: The Hearings Begin

33. Quoted in Bryan F. Le Beau, *The Story of the Salem Witch Trials*. Upper Saddle River, NJ: Prentice-Hall, 1998, p. 68.

34. Quoted in Hill, *A Delusion of Satan*, p. 43.

35. Quoted in Hill, *A Delusion of Satan*, p. 46.

36. Quoted in Hill, *A Delusion of Satan*, p. 48.

37. Quoted in Chadwick Hansen, *Witchcraft at Salem*. New York: Braziller, 1969, p. 37.

38. Quoted in Gragg, *The Salem Witch Crisis*, p. 52.

39. Marion Lena Starkey, *The Devil in Massachusetts: A Modern Enquiry into the Salem Witch Trials*. New York: Doubleday, 1969, p. 58.

40. Quoted in Charles W. Upham, *Salem Witchcraft, with an Account of Salem Village and a History of Opinions on Witchcraft and Kindred Subjects,* Volume II, Boston, MA: Wiggin and Lunt,1867, p. 25.

41. Quoted in Hansen, *Witchcraft at Salem*, p. 37.

42. Quoted in Starkey, *The Devil in Massachusetts*, p. 73.

43. Birnes and Martin, *The Haunting of America*, p. 80.

44. Starkey, *The Devil in Massachusetts*, p. 75.

45. Quoted in Starkey, *The Devil in Massachusetts*, p. 81.

46. Quoted in John Demos, *The Enemy Within: 2,000 Years of Witch-Hunting in the Western World*. New York: Viking, 2008, p. 143.

47. Quoted in Demos, *The Enemy Within*, p. 144.

48. Quoted in Starkey, *The Devil in Massachusetts*, pp. 82, 83.

49. Quoted in Demos, *The Enemy Within*, p. 148.

50. Le Beau, *The Story of the Salem Witch Trials*, p. 91.

51. Quoted in Le Beau, *The Story of the Salem Witch Trials*, p. 91.

52. Rapley, *Witch Hunts*, p. 79

53. Starkey, *The Devil in Massachusetts*, p. 75.

54. Quoted in Hill, *A Delusion of Satan*, p. 100.

Chapter Four: Trials and Punishments

55. Quoted in Le Beau, *The Story of the Salem Witch Trials*, p. 155.
56. Quoted in William Frederick Poole, *Cotton Mather and Salem Witchcraft*. Cambridge: Cambridge University Press, 1869, p. 30.
57. Quoted in Starkey, *The Devil in Massachusetts*, p. 153.
58. Quoted in Le Beau, *The Story of the Salem Witch Trials*, p. 168.
59. Hill, *A Delusion of Satan*, p. 1.
60. Quoted in Hill, *A Delusion of Satan*, p. 174.
61. Quoted in Starkey, *The Devil in Massachusetts*, p. 204.
62. Robert J. Allison, *Before 1776: Life in the American Colonies* (Audio Lecture #19). Chantilly, VA: Teaching Company, 2009.
63. Quoted in Douglas Linder, "The Witchcraft Trials in Salem: A Commentary," University of Missouri–Kansas City. http://law.umkc.edu.
64. Quoted in Hill, *A Salem Witch Reader*, p. 103.

Chapter Five: What Is the Legacy of the Salem Witch Trials?

65. Quoted in Hill, *A Delusion of Satan*, p. 96.
66. Diane E. Foulds, *Death in Salem: The Private Lives Behind the 1692 Witch Hunt*. Guilford, CT: Globe Pequot, 2010, p. 253.
67. Quoted in Demos, *The Enemy Within*, p. 192.
68. Quoted in Demos, *The Enemy Within*, p. 185.
69. Quoted in Gragg, *The Salem Witch Crisis*, p. 202.
70. Hill, *A Delusion of Satan*, pp. 206–207.
71. Quoted in Hill, *A Delusion of Satan*, p. 207.
72. Quoted in Hill, *A Delusion of Satan*, p. 207.
73. Quoted in Le Beau, *The Story of the Salem Witch Trials*, p. 204.
74. Brian A. Pavlac, *Witch Hunts in the Western World: Persecution and Punishment from the Inquisition Through the Salem Trials*. Westport, CT: Greenwood, 2009, p. 143.
75. Quoted in Le Beau, *The Story of the Salem Witch Trials*, p. 245.
76. Doris Eberhardt, personal interview with the author, February 18, 2011, Minneapolis, MN.
77. Quoted in Richard H. Rovere, *Senator Joe McCarthy*. Berkeley and Los Angeles: University of California Press, 1995, p. 123.

78. Quoted in Douglas T. Miller and Marion Novak, *The Fifties: The Way We Really Were*. Garden City, NY: Doubleday, 1977, p. 29.

79. Quoted in Edwin R. Bayley, *Joe McCarthy and the Press*. Madison: University of Wisconsin Press, 1981, p. 51.

80. Quoted in Attorney General John Ashcroft Testimony Before the House Committee on the Judiciary," September 24, 2001. www .justice.gov.

81. Quoted in Rapley, *Witch Hunts*, p. 209.

82. Rapley, *Witch Hunts*, p. 215.

Important People of the Salem Witch Trials

Bridget Bishop: A gregarious tavern owner who dressed in colorful garb and did not care what others thought of her. As she walked past the town meetinghouse, she glanced at it and a heavy beam fell down, convincing villagers that she had cast a spell on it. She was the first of the accused witches to be executed.

Giles Corey: The husband of convicted witch Martha Corey. He refused to enter a plea of guilty or not guilty to the court, and as a result could not be tried. He was pressed to death, still refusing to enter a plea or say anything to the judges other than to ask for more weight.

Dorcas Good: The four-year-old daughter of accused witch Sarah Good. She was suspected because she had a snake for a pet—an indication to the judges that the snake was a familiar. She spent time in prison with her mother and was so traumatized from the experience that she could never live on her own, according to her father.

Sarah Good: The first to be accused of witchcraft, along with Sarah Osborne. Good, a beggar who lived in Salem, had several children, including Dorcas, who accompanied her to prison. Sarah Good was hanged on July 19, 1692.

Increase Mather: The father of Cotton Mather, he was a highly respected minister and the head of Harvard College. He wrote *Cases of Conscience Concerning Evil Spirits* in 1693, which criticized the practice of using spectral evidence in court.

Rebecca Nurse: An elderly Salem woman who was hanged as a witch. Seemingly the least likely to be accused of any wrongdoing, she did not answer questions put to her by the judges. As it turned out, she was deaf and could not hear them.

Betty Parris: The daughter of Samuel Parris, who, with her cousin Abigail Williams, began having fits and acting strangely after dabbling in magic and fortune-telling with their caregiver, Tituba.

Samuel Parris: The minister of Salem Village's church. Parris was involved in the witch trials from the beginning because his daughter and niece were the first to show signs of being afflicted by witchcraft. Parris also fanned the flames of anti-witch fervor from the pulpit during the trials.

William Phips: The governor of Massachusetts Bay Colony. It was Phips who established the Court of Oyer and Terminer that tried the accused witches in Salem Village. Phips's wife was one of the last to be accused by the afflicted girls of being a witch, though by then no one believed the girls' accusations.

Samuel Sewall: A prominent Boston lawyer and judge. He was chosen to be one of the judges on the Court of Oyer and Terminer. After the trials he publicly apologized for his part in what he deemed a mistake in convicting and sentencing so many people to death.

Mary Sibley: A neighbor of the Parris family. It was Sibley who ordered Tituba to bake the witch cake containing the urine of Betty Parris and Abigail Williams and feed it to the family dog. Samuel Parris was furious with Sibley because he felt that using a witch cake was no better than practicing witchcraft.

Tituba: A young Caribbean woman whom Samuel Parris brought as a slave to Salem Village. She is believed to have played fortune-telling games with Betty Parris and Abigail Williams, which some think caused their strange behavior later. Tituba was tried and jailed. Samuel Parris refused to pay her jail fees, and she was eventually sold to a new master who was willing to pay them.

For Further Research

Books

Gretchen A. Adams, *The Specter of Salem: Remembering the Witch Trials in Nineteenth-Century America*. Chicago: University Of Chicago, 2010.

William J. Birnes and Joel Martin, *The Haunting of America: From the Salem Witch Trials to Harry Houdini*. New York: Doherty, 2009.

John Demos, *The Enemy Within: 2,000 Years of Witch-Hunting in the Western World*. New York: Viking, 2008.

Diane E. Foulds, *Death in Salem: The Private Lives Behind the 1692 Witch Hunt*. Guilford, CT: Globe Pequot, 2010.

Judith Bloom Fradin and Dennis Brindell Fradin, *The Salem Witch Trials*. Tarrytown, NY: Marshall Cavendish Benchmark, 2009.

Kekla Magoon, *The Salem Witch Trials*. Edina, MN: ABDO, 2008.

Philip Margulies and Maxine Rosaler, *The Devil on Trial: Witches, Anarchists, Atheists, Communists, and Terrorists in America's Courtrooms*. Boston: Houghton Mifflin, 2008.

Tim McNeese, *The Cold War and Postwar America, 1946–1963*. New York: Chelsea House, 2010.

Websites

A Brief History of the Salem Witch Trials, Smithsonian Institution (www.smithsonianmag.com/history-archaeology/brief-salem.html). A complete telling of the event, with special emphasis on the social and historical background that led to the trials.

Map of Salem Village: Witchcraft Accusations (http://jefferson.village
.virginia.edu/~bcr/salem/salem.html). This unique site contains an interactive map that shows the locations of the accused witches and their
accusers, as well as major roads, rivers, townships, and households.

National Geographic: Salem Witch-Hunt—Interactive (www.national
geographic.com/salem). Included here are questions and answers about
the trials and individuals, as well as interesting things to see and do in
the town of Salem, Massachusetts, to learn more about the witch trials.

Salem Witch Trials (http://etext.virginia.edu/salem/witchcraft). This
site provides a great assortment of primary source documents, from
trial transcripts to rare books, as well as historical maps of Salem Village. There is also a helpful question-and-answer feature with the town
archivist for Danvers, Massachusetts (formerly Salem Village).

Salem Witch Trials—Learning Adventures (http://school.discovery
education.com/schooladventures/salemwitchtrials). A comprehensive
site with excellent sections on the main individuals involved in the
witch trials, this site also has a section on what life was like in seventeenth-century Salem.

Salem Witch Trials of 1692 (www.witchway.net/times/salemwitch
trials.html). This site contains a readable overview of the events and includes links to partial transcripts of some of the trials, as well as articles
about key figures of the trials, such as Tituba, Sarah Good, Giles Corey,
and Bridget Bishop.

Salem Witch Trials, 1692 (http://law.umkc.edu/faculty/projects/ftrials
/salem/salem.htm). This site contains a wide range of information, including maps, images, transcriptions of trials, biographies of some of
the key individuals involved, and games.

Index

Note: Boldface page numbers indicate illustrations.

Allison, Robert J., 62
Ashcroft, John, 79

Ballard, Elizabeth, 58
Ballard, Joseph, 58
Beard, George, 69
Bible
   devils/agents of evil in, 31
   on witchcraft, 32
Birnes, William J., 29
Bishop, Bridget, 55–56, **56**
Branch, Katherine, 72
Briggs, Robin, 11
Burroughs, George, 50, 64
Bush, George W., 79

Calef, Robert, 30
Cary, Elizabeth, 59
Cary, Nathaniel, 59
Cases of Conscience Concerning Evil Spirits (Increase Mather), 72
Charlotte (NC) *Observer* (newspaper), 77
Cheever, Ezekiel, 39
children, Puritan views on rearing, 18–19
Church of England, 12–13
Clark, Peter, 72
Clawson, Elizabeth, 72
Cloyse, Sarah, 49–50
Cold War, 73
confessions, of witches, 58–60
Corey, Giles, 61–62
Corey, Martha, 44–45, 61
Corwin, Jonathan, 39, 50, 53
Court of Oyer and Terminer, 53, 55
   termination of, 62
The Crucible (Miller), 75

A Delusion of Satan (Hill), 19–20, 41
The Devil in Massachusetts (Starkey), 35
Disborough, Mercy, 72

Easty, Mary, 60–61
Eberhardt, Doris, 74

Endecott, John, 20
Erikson, Kai T., 37
evidence, spectral, 54, 55
  end of, 70–72
executions, 28, 55–56, 57–58
  numbers of, 11, 66

familiars/animal companions,
  15, 23
Feingold, Russ, 80
Foulds, Diane E., 67

Gedney, Bartholomew, 53
Glover, Goody, 25–26
Good, Dorcas, 48, 66
Good, Sarah, 36–37, 56–57,
  66
  magistrate hearing on,
    39–40
Good, William, 66
Goodwin, John, 25
Goodwin, Martha, 26
Griggs, William, 32
Guantánamo Bay Naval Base
  (Cuba), 79

Hale, John, 29–30, 30–31, 62,
  69
Hathorne, John, 49, 53
  examination of Sarah Good
    by, 39–40

examination of Tituba by,
  42–43
  in hearing on Sarah Nurse,
    46–47
Hathorne, William, 48
Hawthorne, Nathaniel, 49
Henry VIII (king of England),
  12
Hibbins, Anne, 25
Higginson, John, 48
Hill, Frances, 17–18, 34, 59
  on hanging of George
    Burroughs, 64
  on punishment, 21
  on Puritans' view of religious
    freedom, 19–20
  on remorse in aftermath of
    trials, 70
  on testimony of Deodat
    Lawson, 41
  on torture of the accused, 60
House Committee on
  Un-American Activities
  (HCUA), 74
Hubbard, Elizabeth, 36
Hutchinson, Joseph, 37
hysteria, 67, 69

Indian, John, 28, 32, 34

jails, 51–52, 54
James I (king of England), 13

Janeway, James, 18–19

Kamensky, Jane, 15–16

Lawson, Deodat, 31
  testimony of, 41

Malleus Maleficarum (Hammer of Witches), 10
Martin, Joel, 29
Massachusetts, c. 1692, **9**
Massachusetts Bay Colony, 13, 20
Mather, Cotton, 19, 26, **27**, 64
  on alternative punishment, 54–55
  on evidence allowed in court, 54
Mather, Increase, 72
McCarthy, Joseph, 75–78, **77**
Miller, Arthur, 75
More Wonders of the Invisible World (Calef), 30

Nurse, Rebecca, 45–47, 48, 60
  trial of, 56–57

Osborne, Alexander, 37
Osborne, Sarah, 37

death of, 52
magistrate hearing on, 40, 41

Parris, Betty, 28, 29, 30–31, 36
  behavior of, 35
  testimony of, 40
  Tituba and, 28–30
Parris, Samuel, 28, 30, 47, 49, 69
  on the devil, 31–32
  on Mary Sibley, 34–36
  on witch cake, 34–36
PATRIOT Act. *See* USA PATRIOT Act
Pavlac, Brian, 72
Phips, William, 53–54, 64–65
Preston, Thomas, 37
Proctor, Elizabeth, 49, 50
Proctor, John, 48–49, 50
The Psychology of the Salem Witchcraft Excitement of 1692 (Beard), 69
Puritans/Puritanism, 11, **17**
  beliefs of, 9, 14–18
  children and, 18–19
  Church of England and, 12–13
  punishments imposed by, 20–23, **22**, **32**
  theocracy established by, 13
  views on conformity, 20–21
  views on Quakers, 20

views on religious freedom,
19–20
Putnam, Ann, 36, 46, 50, 58
Putnam, Edward, 37
Putnam, Thomas, 37

al Qaeda, 78
Quakers, 20

Rapley, Robert, 24, 47, 80
Ratcliff, Philip, 22
Remy, Nicholas, 10–11
Richards, John, 53, 54
Rogers, Horatio, 20
Rovere, Richard H., 76

Salem Village, Massachusetts,
51
establishment of, 14
first accusations of witchcraft
in, 36–37
first threats of witchcraft in,
25
founders of, 9
life in, 16–18
The Salem Witch Trials Reader
(Hill), 64
Saltonstall, Nathaniel, 53,
56
The Scarlet Letter
(Hawthorne), 49

September 11 attacks (2001),
witch hunt following, 78–80
Sergeant, Peter, 53
Sewall, Samuel, 16, 17, 53, 70
Shepard, Thomas, 18
Sibley, Mary
witch cake and, 32, 33,
35–36
Soviet Union/Communism,
73–74
Starkey, Marion Lena, 35, 42,
45, 48
Stoughton, William, 53, 55, 57

theocracy, 13
Tituba, 32, 34, 36, 37, **43**
confession of, 42–44
influence of, on Abigail
Williams/Betty Parris,
28–30, 69
A Token for Children
(Janeway), 19
torture, 60, 62, **63**, 79, 80
Truman, Harry, 74

USA PATRIOT Act (2001),
79–80

Walcott, Mary, 58
Warren, Mary, 48, 50
Wayward Puritans (Erikson), 37

Weisman, Richard, 10
Wiesel, Elie, 75
Willard, Samuel, 9
Williams, Abigail, 28–29,
    30–31, 36
  Deodat Lawson on behavior
    of, 31
  testimony of, 40
  Tituba and, 28–30
Winthrop, John, 13–14
Winthrop, Wait Still, 53
witch cakes, 32, 34
witches, **68**
  accused, apologies to, 70
  accused, confessions of,
    58–69

animal companions/
    familiars of, 15, 23, **45**
belief in, 10, 31
executions of, 57–58
hysteria and, 67, 69
methods of determining
    guilt of, 29, 32–33
swimming of, 29
Witches and Neighbours
    (Briggs), 11
witch hunts
  after 9/11 attacks,
    78–80
  of Cold War era, 73–78
  in Europe, 10–11
  during world War II, 71

Picture Credits

Cover: The Trial of George Jacobs, 5th August 1692, 1855 (oil on canvas), Matteson, Tompkins Harrison (1813-84) / © Peabody Essex Museum, Salem, Massachusetts, USA / The Bridgeman Art Library

© Bettmann/Corbis: 56, 63, 77

© Lake County Museum/Corbis: 45

© Northwind Picture Archives: 17, 22, 27, 33, 43, 68

Thinkstock/iStockphoto.com: 6, 7

Steve Zmina: 9, 51

About the Author

Gail B. Stewart is the award-winning author of more than 250 books for children and young adults. She is the mother of three grown sons and lives in Minneapolis, Minnesota.